THE VAIŚEṢIKA THEORY OF KNOWLEDGE

(According to Praśastapada)

THE VAIŚEṢIKA THEORY OF KNOWLEDGE

(According to Praśastapada)

Dr. Jhumur Mallik

MAHA BODHI BOOK AGENCY
4A, Bankim Chatterjee Street, College Square
Kolkata - 700 073, INDIA
2017

THE VAIŚEṢIKA THEORY OF KNOWLEDGE

(According to Praśastapada)

By

Dr. Jhumur Mallik

First Published 2017

Published by :

D.L.S. Jayawardana

MAHA BODHI BOOK AGENCY

4-A, Bankim Chatterjee Street, College Square
Kolkata-700 073 (India)
Phone : 9831077368, 9831529452
Email : mahabodhibookagency@hotmail.com

Printed by :

Sagarika Press, Kolkata-700 009

ISBN : 978-93-84721-76-3

Price : ₹ 400.00

Preface

The Padārthadharmasaṅgraha or Praśastapādabhāṣya is perhaps the most important and authoritative text on the ancient Vaiśeṣika system of philosophy. But it appears that it has not received much attention from the scholars and to the best of our knowledge it has not been critically studied either as a whole or partially. In our opinion it is very difficult to make a critical study of the whole work within the expanse of a single work. I have therefore selected as the subject of my study a special topic, namely, the Vaiśeṣika theory of knowledge as presented by Praśastapāda.

I am grateful to Dr. Sarbani Ganguli, (Retd.) Professor of Sanskrit, Jadavpur University, Kolkata and Professor Mrinal Kanti Gangopadhyay, (Retd.) Asutosh Professor of Sanskrit, Calcutta University, who have consented to act as my advisers. They have extended all necessary help to me. They have devoted a lot of time in explaining the subject clearly to me. They have also provided me with valuable suggestions for the improvement of the study.

Naturally, I have received help from the works of various authors. I record my indebtedness to all of them.

I am also thankful to Rupali Dutta for helping me to correct the proof.

Jhumur Mallik

Preface

Contents

CHAPTER ONE

Valid Knowledge and Its Forms

According to the Indian tradition, all the systems of philosophy (*darśana*) represent what is known as *mokṣaśastra*. The ultimate end of all the systems is to lead one to final liberation, which is the highest aim of human existence (*parama-puruṣārtha*). But how is this aim to be achieved? The Vaiśeṣika answers that the highest good can be attained by the right knowledge of categories (*padārtha*) through the consideration of their similarities and dissimilarities.[1] Hence it follows that the problem of knowledge should find an important place in the Vaiśeṣika philosophy. Besides, every system has its own metaphysics and it can be properly established and defended only on the basis of a sound theory of knowledge.

But an enquiry into the conditions of valid thought and the methods of valid knowledge presupposes an account of the nature and forms of cognition or knowledge in general. It requires us also to consider the nature and method of valid knowledge in general and the nature and test of truth or validity in particular. The philosopher of a particular school has thus to find answers to such questions as: What is cognition or knowledge as such? What are its different forms? What is valid knowledge? What is meant by a method of valid knowledge in general? What do we mean by truth or validity? What is the test of truth, the measure of true knowledge, the standard of validity? What are the constituents or factors of valid knowledge?

Naturally, like all the other systems, the Vaiśeṣika also has offered its own answers to such questions. Though it is true that from a very ancient time the Vaiśeṣika has been closely related with the Nyāya, both advocating the atomic theory and many other things in common and in course of time the two become actually amalgamated, still, so far as the theory of knowledge is concerned, they do not perhaps follow, at least in the earlier phase, the same tradition. We shall have an opportunity to elaborate the point later. For the present we can only mention the fact that while Nyāya admits four *pramāṇas*,[2] Vaiśeṣika admits only two and moreover, even regarding the nature of perception and inference there are some fundamental differences.

Here we have also to note another fact. An early account, reliable and informative, of the Vaiśeṣika theories is not easily available. The work of Kaṇāda, supposed to be the original text of the system, is not a systematic one. There is also much dispute regarding the number, order and actual readings of the *sūtras*. The topics are also not treated clearly and in sufficient details. In fact, the only dependable work of the early Vaiśeṣika that has come down to us is the *Praśastapādabhāṣya* or *Padārthadharmasaṅgraha.*[3] In this work the author has discussed systematically and in great details the Vaiśeṣika theory of knowledge.

However, for a better understanding of the Vaiśeṣika position it is also necessary to have a general idea of the tradition in this regard as prevalent in the various systems of Indian philosophy.

Characteristics of Valid Knowledge.

It is more or less agreed that the word *pramāṇa* is derived in the sense of the instrumental (*karaṇa-vācya*) and therefore it stands for an instrument of a valid cognition. But naturally there are differences of opinion regarding the exact nature of this instrument and the systems are also not unanimous about the nature of a valid cognition. We shall try to have an idea about the various characteristics of valid knowledge as advocated by the different systems of Indian philosophy.

The first and foremost characteristic of a valid knowledge which is equally accepted by all the systems is non-contradictedness (*abādhitatva*). A cognition to be valid must not be negated by a subsequent cognition. When one cognises a rope as rope the cognition is not subsequently set aside. But when one cognises a rope as snake it is later set aside by the awareness that it is not a snake or that it is only a rope. A true cognition is that which informs us of the existence of something in a place where it really exists, or which predicates of something a character really possessed by it.

Another characteristic of valid knowledge is that it must be a definite categorical awareness as distinguished from all indefinite, problematic and hypothetical knowledge. In the case of such knowledge there is a feeling of assurance and conviction in what is known. In other words, valid knowledge is always connected with a firm belief. Thus it excludes such forms of invalid knowledge as doubt (*saṃśaya*) and hypothetical argument (*tarka*). Of course, in the case of illusion also we have a definite knowledge. Still it does not constitute valid knowledge, because it does not share the first essential characteristic mentioned above.

The Position of Bhāṭṭa Mīmāṃsā.

Another characteristic of valid knowledge is said to be novelty (*anādhigatatva*), though all the systems are not unanimous on this point. Some consider it to be an essential characteristic of knowledge, but others consider it unnecessary on the ground that it unduly narrows the scope of knowledge.

According to the Bhāṭṭa school of Mīmāṃsā, valid knowledge is defined as primary and original knowledge[4]. A source of knowledge is that which gives us new knowledge, i.e. a true cognition of objects of which we have had no knowledge in the past. Every case of knowledge, if it is to be of any value should be original in character. It implies a new step by which we advance from the known to what is not yet known. A source of knowledge is the means for acquiring knowledge, and it should lead to the acquisition of such knowledge as is not yet attained, but is still to be acquired. If an object is already known, there can be no necessity of acquiring a knowledge of it once more.

It is asked, what is the purpose to be served by a source of knowledge in respect of an object already known by another source of knowledge? The specific result to be obtained by the operation of a source of knowledge is nothing but a correct awareness about an object. When such an awareness is already obtained by the operation of one source of knowledge, the employment of another source of knowledge becomes redundant.

One may argue that it may be necessary to know once again an object already known, because knowledge is the cause of practical activity (*vyavahāra*). The awareness of the object which has been acquired earlier is not present subsequently. For the subsequent practical activity in respect of the object it would be necessary to have a subsequent awareness of the same. A future practical activity is not possible on the basis of a past awareness. Thus for explaining the succeeding activities in later and later times, it would be necessary to know an object again and again in different times.

The Bhāṭṭas however reject the contention. They point out that the first awareness of an object produces an impression (*saṃskāra*) and subsequently a series of recollections (*smṛti-santati*) may be produced from it and the later practical activities in respect of the object may proceed from the subsequent recollections. The recollection of an object previously known and an awareness of an object by a source of knowledge which has already been known by some other source of knowledge has the same status. Both of them reveal what has already been revealed.[5]

Moreover, *pramāṇa* is defined to be the instrumental cause of *pramā*, which means that *pramāṇa* is a special kind of cause, namely, the most efficient (*sādhakatama*) one of the causes. *Pramā* is the thing to be accomplished (*sādhya*) and *pramāṇa* is the most efficient means for its accomplishment. When the thing to be accomplished is actually accomplished by some means, one does not have any scope for employing another means for the same. The desire for employing a means persists so long as the purpose is not accomplished. One employs the axe so long as the act of cutting is not accomplished. It is not employed in respect of what is already cut into pieces. Therefore, to know an object already known would be as useless as grinding the ground (*piṣṭta-peṣaṇa*). It also suffers from the defect of *kalpanā-gaurava*.[6]

Objections Against The Bhatta View.

According to Nyāya, however novelty cannot be regarded as an essential character of knowledge. In that case, the definition becomes too narrow, because a number of valid cognitions would remain outside the scope of *pramā*. For example, it would not be possible to justify the validity of re-cognition (*pratyabhijñā*).[7] To re-cognise a thing is to know it as what was once known before. In the case of such knowledge, the object that is perceived at present is directly felt as the same one that was perceived in the past. When we have, for example, an awareness, in the form 'this is that man whom I saw yesterday' the *this* of the present perception is identified with the *that* of the past perception. Re-cognition cannot therefore be a knowledge of what is not previously known. Still, it is admitted as a form of valid knowledge.

We may note here briefly the different views about the nature of re-cognition as held by the philosophers of the different schools.

The Buddhist cannot naturally accept re-cognition as a *pramāṇa*, because, being an advocate of momentariness, he dismisses as unreal all permanence, which is what is supposed to constitute the object of re-cognition. Moreover, according to him, it is not one single piece of cognition but a combination of two pieces of cognition, namely, perception and memory, given one name. In such awareness, the element of *that* cannot be an object of perception and hence becomes an object of memory. The element of *this*, on the other hand, can be an object of perception and is not an object of any non-perceptual cognition.

But systems like Nyāya, Mīmāṃsā and others maintain that re-cognition is one single piece of cognition. There is no doubt a general rule to the effect that the object of perception must be a present entity, but an exception to the rule has to be made when certain particular causal aggregate is present. Thus, for example, Vācaspati says that sense-organs which generally grasp only present entities, succeed in producing re-cognition, because with impression (*saṃskāra*) or memory acting as an accessory they become capable of grasping a present entity as qualified by a past state.[8] It is moreover argued that there is no ground to reject the validity of such knowledge. In fact, it is considered by them as the decisive evidence for rejecting momentariness and defending the permanence of things.

The Jainas agree with the others systems on the two main points, namely, re-cognition is a single piece of knowledge and it has validity, but differ in explaining its nature. With them, it is a type of non-perceptual cognition (*parokṣa-jñāna*) and they are of the view that in the wake of sense-perception and memory, there arises a mental cognition of a special type that takes cognizance of two entities as somehow related to each other. This mental cognition is recognition.[9]

But the most serious charge against the inclusion of novelty in the definition of *pramā* is that the definition would not then apply to what is called a continuous cognition (*dhārāvāhika-jñāna*).[10] When the same thing is known by one for sometime, there is a series of continuous cognitions revealing the thing. There all the cognitions, which follow the first one and constitute the series, refer to the same thing as has been already known by the first cognition. It cannot be said that each member of the series refers to a new object. Thus when one keeps looking at a table for some moments continuously, one's experience of the first moment, being an awareness of a thing previously unknown, may be called valid knowledge. But what would be the status of the cognitions acquired in the subsequent moments? They should not be regarded as valid as they lack the quality of novelty. But the fact is they cannot be rejected as invalid, because they definitely share the primary quality of non-contradictedness.

Of course, the Bhāṭṭas deny the charge and argue that there is no such difficulty in the case of a continuous cognition. Each member of the cognition-series is produced at different moments of time and the object is not the same at different moments, though it may ordinarily appear to be so.[11] Even if it is granted that the same object persists without any spatial change for a certain period, yet the inevitable temporal change has to be taken into consideration. In other words, an object of knowledge is determined both spatially and temporally to our consciousness. By perceiving its spatial properties we judge it to be big or small, red or blue. Similarly, by perceiving its temporal property we judge it to be present or past. Without perceiving this time-quality it would be difficult for us to distinguish the present knowledge of an object or its perception from the past knowledge of the object or its memory. Thus an object as determined by the first moment of a continuous cognition is not the same as determined by the second moment. Every moment we have the knowledge of an object that is different from the object of the previous moment and is therefore as good as a new object. The, definition of valid cognition can thus apply to it without any difficulty.

View of Advaita Vedāntins

In a later work discussing the Advaita Vedānta theory of knowledge the question concerning the validity of a continuous cognition has been sought to be explained in a different way.[12] According to the author, the problem or difficulty as pointed out above simply does not arise and it is not therefore necessary to offer any defence for or explanation as solving it. It is maintained that a cognition persists so long as a fresh cognition does not come to replace it. A cognition is to be regarded as a single piece of knowledge as long as no new mental modification is produced and it continues to be there whether a cognition changes or remains the same can only be ascertained by determining whether the logical activity of the self, i.e. the judgement affirming the knowledge (e.g. the pot is or the pot is perceived) changes or remains the same.

Those who raise the above problem do so on the assumption that in a continuous cognition there are separate pieces of knowledge every moment during the period of persistence, while the content or object of these distinct pieces of knowledge is the same and therefore at every subsequent moment there is only a repetition or reproduction of the knowledge of the first moment. But this assumption is wrong. If the object of the so called different pieces of knowledge is admitted to be identical, they are themselves indistinguishable from each other, i.e. they actually represent only one identical process of knowledge. The question of repetition or reproduction does not arise at all.

The Nyāya Position

The Naiyāyikas who strongly advocate the view that novelty cannot be considered an essential property of a valid cognition find fault with the explanation given by the Bhāṭṭas and the Advaita Vedāntins. They point out that an instant of time (*kṣaṇa*) cannot be perceived by us.[13] Time is not a perceptible substance and moreover, an instant of time is too minute. Thus the different instants cannot be said to enter into the continuous cognition and constitute different objects for the individual members of a series of cognitions. If these temporal differences were really apprehended and went inseparably into the body of the continuous cognition, its continuity would have been broken up and our sense of continuity would have been lost. But this is not actually the case. Therefore, it is to be accepted that in a continuous cognition all the individual cognitions refer to one and the same object.

It can neither be argued that a continuous cognition is a single state of cognition enduring for sometime. From a subjective standpoint it may be considered to be one present state of conscious illumination, yet objectively it is a series of cognitions. The present is not a point or one instant of time, which is imperceptible, but a mass or block comprising several instants, while a cognition cannot endure for more than one moment or instant of time. Hence a continuous cognition is really a series of cognitions of which those that succeed the first are admitted to be as valid as the first. It cannot be said that they reveal newer and newer aspects of the object. As Jayanta remarks, the palm of the hand seen thousandth time adds no new content to our previous knowledge of it.[14]

In fact, the validity of knowledge is not in any way dependent upon novelty. No knowledge is made true or false simply because it is original or unoriginal. The validity of a cognition consists in three aspects, namely, first, a correct presentation of the object; secondly, the practical activity of the knower in response to it, and finally, fulfillment of the activity in relation to the object. These three facts are inseparably connected with one another and with the true presentation of an object there follows a reaction according to the nature of the object (desirable or undesirable) and the fulfillment of the reaction by way of its producing the expected results. All the repeated experiences of a thing are equally connected with these three facts. Hence, there is no ground to reject the validity of the subsequent cognitions and novelty is not really a mark of valid knowledge.[15]

Some Other Views

While the followers of Kumārila justify the validity of continuous cognition by admitting the awareness of minute divisions of time, the followers of Prabhākara do so without admitting such awareness. They argue that all the individual cognitions in a continuous cognition are independent of one another; neither for their origin nor for their awareness are they mutually dependent. Moreover, they are all presentative knowledge (*anubhava*).[16] Therefore, a continuous cognition should be considered valid. This position agrees with that of the Nyāya.

In the Buddhist tradition we do not find any specific reference to this problem of validity regarding a continuous cognition, though we can have some idea from the statements of some of the commentators. While explaining the nature of right knowledge, Dharmottara[17] clearly maintains that novelty should be considered as one of its essential characteristics. The first awareness leads one to activity and one obtains the desired object. A subsequent awareness can do nothing more. Hence the first awareness or the awareness which reveals an object which is not revealed before should alone be accepted as valid. This contention seems to suggest that he is not inclined to treat a continuous cognition as valid.

Another commentator, Arcaṭa,[18] in his commentary on the *Hetubindu* has, incidentally but clearly, formulated his view on the question of continuous cognition being valid or not. He maintains that the continuous cognition of a *yogin* is valid, because it can involve awareness of minute divisions of time, but an ordinary person's continuous cognition is not valid because it does not involve any such awareness. In other words, the validity of such a cognition depends on the nature of the knower. This position is similar to that of Kumārila so far as awareness of minute time-divisions is concerned. But Kumārila does not accept a *yogin* with extraordinary powers and claims that such awareness is possible in the case of ordinary persons also.

Coming to the Jaina tradition, we find that the texts follow either of the traditions. Here also they stick to some of their own peculiar doctrines. Thus, according to the Digambara tradition,[19] a continuous cognition is valid only when it takes note of specialities (*viśeṣa*) like moments (*kṣaṇa*) etc. and thus produces every moment the knowledge of newly specialised objects; but if it takes no such note of specialities, it is not valid. It is further maintained that such a cognition, even while producing the knowledge of specialized object, is not valid so far as the substance-aspect (*dravyāṃśa*) is concerned, because it produces no specialised knowledge concerning this aspect, but is valid so far as the speciality aspect is concerned, because it does produce specialised knowledge concerning this aspect. In other words, the same piece of cognition may be valid or invalid according to the nature of its object.

On the other hand, scholars following the Śvetāmbara tradition are unanimous in considering continuous cognition as valid just like memory (*smṛti*). Accordingly, they also do not subscribe to the view that the object of a valid knowledge should necessarily be hitherto unknown or novel. Thus, according to them, a continuous cognition is valid in its own right. It is not invalid, though it reveals an object already known. Nor should we try to justify its validity by assigning some special sort of object to it.

Valid Knowledge in Nyāya Works

With this general idea of the nature of valid knowledge as discussed by the different schools of Indian philosophy, let us now see briefly how the topic has been treated in some of the authoritative works of Nyāya.

Gautama himself does not offer any general definition of either *pramāṇa* or *pramā*, though he speaks of four kinds of *pramāṇas*, and defines and discusses the four types of *pramā*. In some of the statements of Vātsyāyana, however, we find some hint as to what is to be regarded as validity of knowledge.

Before entering into the actual explanation of the *sūtras*, Vātsyāyana adds an introduction of his own in which he begins with the very defence of *pramāṇa*, establishing the fact that it is possible to ascertain the validity of a piece of cognition. According to him, it can be done by inference and the inference specifically is: *pramāṇam arthavat pravṛtti–sāmarthyāt*. The term standing here for the inferable property (*sādhya*), namely, *arthavat*, is significant.

Vācaspati Miśra has brought out its significance.[20] He says that the suffix *matup* in the term is in the special sense of *nityayoga*. But the question is how are we to dissolve the compound in the expression *nityayoga*? First, it may be taken as a *tatpuruṣa* compound with the sixth case-ending, *nityayor yogaḥ*, i.e. a relation between two eternal things. But this meaning is not acceptable in the present context. In some rare case a *pramāṇa* and its object may both be eternal, but generally the case is just the opposite.

Secondly, the compound may be regarded as a *karmadhārāya*, *nityo yogaḥ*, i.e. an eternal relation. According to Nyāya, such a relation would be none other than the relation of inherence (*samavāya*). But this meaning also cannot be accepted. The relation of inherence is possible only in certain specific cases and a *pramāṇa* and its object are not mutually related through inherence. Vācaspati Miśra, therefore, comments that by eternality (*nityata*) we are to understand non-deviation (*avyabhicārita*). *Pramāṇa* is said to be *arthavat* because of the fact that it is non-deviating in respect of its object.

It is further pointed out that even then there may be an objection. This meaning also is not really applicable in the present case. The term non-deviation actually means a relation of being the pervader and the pervaded (*vyāpya-vyāpaka-bhāva*). But there is no such relation between a *pramāṇa* and a *prameya* or *vice versa*. Vācaspati Miśra, therefore, specifies the exact meaning of non-deviation here in the following terms: an object as proved to be of a specific nature by a *pramāṇa* is never found to be otherwise even in a different time, place and condition, and this non-contradiction (*avisaṃvāda*) between the object and its presentation by a *pramana* constitutes non-deviation.[21] In short, a valid knowledge, is capable of revealing an object as it actually is (*bhūtārtha-paricchedaka*). Thus we get the first essential characteristic of valid knowledge, namely, non-contradictedness.

The View of Uddyotakara

Vatsyayana has explained that a general definition of *pramāṇa* is available from the grammatical analysis of the term itself.[22] A *pramāṇa* is the instrument for acquiring an awareness (*upalabdhi*). Following this line of interpretation Uddyotakara defines *pramāṇa* as the cause of awareness (*upalabdhi-hetu*).[23] But the term *upalabdhi* stands for any kind of awareness irrespective of whether it is valid or false. In that case the instrument of each and every awareness would have to be considered a *pramāṇa*. But this is not an acceptable position. A doubt (*saṃśaya*) or a contradictory cognition (*viparyāsa*) also represents a kind of awareness, but the instrument producing either of them is not accepted as a *pramāṇa*.

In answer, it is pointed out that the term *arthavat* is to be added to the definition and thus, the implication would be that an instrument would be a *pramāṇa* only when it gives rise to an awareness which has invariable connection with its object. A doubt or a contradictory cognition, though a form of awareness, is not invariably connected with its object. The former points to an object as sharing two opposite characteristics, e.g. a thing is presented as a post or as a human being. But an object characterised by the properties of both does not exist anywhere. Similarly, an object is presented by the latter as something which it is actually not, e.g. a piece of rope is presented as a snake. None of these two kinds of awareness can lead to any fruitful activity (*artha-kriyā*). Therefore, none has invariable connection with an object.[24]

Doubt Not a Form of Valid Knowledge

From the above it follows that knowledge in the form of doubt is to be excluded from the category of valid knowledge by the addition of the term *arthavat* to the definition as suggested by Uddyotakara. Though all the schools of Indian philosophy are unanimous on the point that doubt is not a form of valid knowledge, there is some difference of opinion as to how it is to be excluded. The simplest way to do so is to start with a classification of knowledge into the two categories of *yathārtha* and *ayathārtha*, and then classify the latter further into various types, one of them being doubt. For example, as we shall later see, Praśastapāda divides knowledge into two classes, *vidyā* and *avidyā* and includes doubt under the latter. But such an enumeration does not point to any ground for excluding doubt from the category of valid knowledge. If the above line of interpretation is followed an answer is possible, namely, just like illusion, doubt also is deviating in respect of its object and hence it is included in invalid knowledge. This line of thinking seems to be accepted by the Bhaṭṭas also, when they insist that a valid knowledge must reveal a real object (*tattvārtha*).[25]

However, some authorities exclude doubt by expressly adding a clause that valid knowledge is something other than doubt (*asandigdha*). Jayanta Bhaṭṭa, for example, subscribes to such a view.[26] Vācaspati Miśra in his *Tattvakaumudī* also explains the definition of valid knowledge in the same way.[27] Commentators point out that though it is true that in many cases a doubt refers to an object which is contradicted (*bādhita-viṣayaka*) and as such, it may be treated as a case of error (*viparyaya*), there may be some cases of doubt which are not so (*bhrametara*). For example, a doubt in the form: Is or is not the tree characterised by conjunction-with–monkey (*kapi-saṃyoga*)?

This doubt consists of two alternatives: (i) the tree is characterised by conjunction-with–monkey and (ii) the tree is not characterised by conjunction-with-monkey. One of these alternatives is true and hence, the doubt cannot be simply declared to be an error. Thus, at least partly, it may be said to point to a real object just like a piece of valid knowledge. So that even such a doubt is not included in the category of *pramā*, it is necessary to add the clause 'something other than doubt.'[28]

Evidence of The Nyāyasūtra.

In this connection, it would perhaps be interesting and relevant to note how the commentators of Gautama explain the significance of the term *avyabhicārin* in the definition of perception given by him. According to Vātsyāyana, the term is included to exclude a case of perceptual error. Thus he says:[29]

"During the summer the flickering rays of the sun intermingle with the heat radiating from the surface of the earth come in contact with the visual organ of a person at a distance. Due to this sense-object contact, there arises, in the rays of the sun, the awareness that it is water. Even such an awareness may be taken for a valid perceptual knowledge. Hence, (Gautama) says 'invariably connected with the object'. An erroneous perception is the perception of an object as something which it is not. A right perception is the perception of an object as it actually is."

According to him, the applicability of the definition to doubt is prevented by a different term, namely, of a definite character (*vyavasāyātmaka*).[30] Doubt is not excluded by the former term. Since Vātsyāyana says that a right perception is the perception of an object as it actually is, a doubt also may be considered non–deviating.

The idea may be explained as follows. On perceiving for example, the common characteristics of dust and smoke in a distant object, one has the doubt, is it dust or is it smoke? If the object is really dust the awareness is non-erroneous in its first part and if the object is really smoke, the perception is non-erroneous in its second part. Since the object is either dust or smoke, the awareness may be said to be invariably related to the object or non-deviating. So it is necessary to exclude doubt by a different term.

Therefore, Vātsyāyana contends that the term *vyavasāyātmaka*, of a definite character, has been added by Gautama to exclude doubt form the category of valid perception. So he remarks : "On perceiving with the eyes an object at a distance, a person cannot decide whether it is smoke or dust. As such, an indecisive knowledge (*anavadhāraṇa–jñāna)* resulting from sense-object contact may be taken for perceptual knowledge. Hence, (Gautaṃa) says 'of a definite character'[31]

Of course, it may be pointed out that, strictly speaking, non-deviation should be considered a property of valid knowledge in general and not of perception only. It may therefore be asked what is the need for the use of the word *avyabhicārin* in the definition of perception to exclude cases of error? Perception is already admitted to be a form of *pramā* and by definition it should be non-deviating or non-illusory. Cases of error will be automatically excluded from the category of *pramā*. Moreover, even if the term be included in the definition of perception, it should also be included, on the same ground, in the definitions of all the other forms of valid knowledge like inference and others. But the fact is that Gautama has not done so.[32]

The point does not escape the notice of Vācaspati Miśra. After some discussions he answers that actually the non-deviation of all the other forms of valid knowledge is derived from the non-deviation of perception, which ultimately lies at the root of them. All the forms of valid knowledge are indirectly dependent upon perception and if this perception is deviating they also cannot be non-deviating. Gautama uses the word *avyabhicārin* in definition of perception only to indicate this speciality of perception. In support of his contention, he also quotes the authority of Kumārila Bhaṭṭa.[33]

Position of Vācaspati

While giving the definition of valid knowledge in the *Tattvakaumudī*, Vācaspati Miśra adds two separate terms, namely, *asandigdha* and *aviparīta* to exclude doubt and error respectively. But while explaining Gautama's definition he does not agree with Vātsyāyana that doubt and error are excluded by two separate terms, but argues that the single term *avyabhicārin* excludes not only error but also doubt. He contends that a knowledge in the form of doubt cannot actually lead to the attainment of an object as indicated (*vikalpyamāna*) by the knowledge. Since it cannot make one attain what is pointed to it cannot be considered as corresponding to reality (*saṃvādaka*) and since it is not *saṃvādaka*, it cannot also be considered *avyabhicārin*. Thus, both doubt and error are excluded by the same term.[34]

What, then, is the significance of the term *vyavasāyātmaka*? It is used to indicate the fact that, according to Gautama, determinate perception also is a kind of valid knowledge, though it is not accepted as valid by the Buddhists. In fact, according to Vācaspati, Gautama gives not only the definition of perception but also refers to its classification. The terms *avyapadeśya* and *vyavasāyātmaka* respectively indicate the two forms of perception admitted by Nyāya, namely, indeterminate (*nirvikalpaka*) and determinate (*savikalpaka*). The rest of the *sūtra* gives the actual definition of perception.[35]

However, it has been pointed out that it is difficult to accept Vācaspati's interpretation. It neither agrees with the views of Vātsyāyana and Uddyotakara nor is it justified by anything in the *sūtra* itself.[36] As a matter of fact Vācaspati's zeal to refute the Buddhist view which does not recognise the validity of determinate perception leads him to see in the *sūtra* a reference to the two forms of perception and this, as he himself mentions clearly, is in accordance with the line of interpretation suggested by his preceptor Trilocana.[37] The famous Jaina logician Hemacandra remarks, in his *Pramāṇamīmāṃsā*, that Trilocana and Vācaspati have evolved a novel explanation of the *sūtra* disregarding the views of the earlier commentators.[38]

It is well known that Jayanta Bhatta, another celebrated commentator of the *Nyāyasūtra*, generally notes and examines exhaustively the various views and interpretations of a term. But in the present case he also does not refer to any different interpretation and himself reiterates exactly what has been said by Vātsyāyana.[39] Moreover, he emphatically argues that a single term cannot exclude both doubt and error, because they are different by nature (*svarūpabheda*) and they are produced by different causes (*kāraṇabheda*). Thus doubt refers unfixedly to more than one alternative, but error refers to a single and definite alternative. Again, doubt is produced by the recollection of the specific characteristics of more than one thing, but error is produced by that of a single thing only. Therefore, different terms are necessary to exclude different forms of cognition.[40]

Doubt : Deviating or Non-deviating?

The argument of those who claim that doubt cannot be excluded by the term *avyabhicārin* is generally that even in the case of doubt one of the alternatives is true and hence, doubt may be considered as non-deviating.[41] The point may be explained further. In the case of error, one single thing is ascribed to another single thing, and when a piece of knowledge negating the wrong awareness is produced the error is removed. But in the case of doubt though two things are ascribed to a single thing the right awareness removing the doubt does not consist of an awareness negating both the things ascribed. The wrong apprehension of a snake in the rope is removed by the awareness 'this is not a snake'. But when there is a doubt in the form (about an object standing at a distance) 'is it a tree or a man' it is removed by, the awareness either 'it is not a tree' or 'it is not a man' (as the actual case may be), and not by an awareness in the form 'it is neither a tree nor a man'.[42] This indicates that an error and a doubt are different by nature .

As against the above, it is pointed out that there can, in fact, be cases of doubt in respect of which such a contention is not true. For example, in the distant field one may be aware of something and have a doubt, is it a snake or a piece of rope? But actually arriving at the spot one may find that it is neither a snake nor a piece of rope, but is really a line showing the crack in the dried up soil. Similarly in the case of something standing in the middle of the distant field one may not decide whether it is a tree or a man but on reaching the spot may find that it is really neither, being really an iron pillar. In such cases a doubt is definitely deviating and can be excluded by the term *avyabhicārin*.[43]

Moreover, doubt though consisting of two alternatives, is a single piece of knowledge and the claim that it is deviating with reference to one part and it is also non-deviating with reference to another part is not justified. In fact, such a claim would lead to the total denial of the particular form of knowledge called doubt itself.[44] For example, in the standard example of a doubt whether the thing standing at a distance is a tree or a man one may argue that if the thing is really a man the knowledge with reference to the second part may be considered as a true ascertainment (*niścaya*) and with reference to the first part it may be considered as an error consisting of one alternative only. In other words, an attempt at defining the character of the knowledge in the case of a doubt by dividing it into separate parts would be illogical. It should rather be admitted as a distinct form of knowledge, without referring to parts, in which the mind oscillates between different alternatives. Thus Udayana, while commenting on the claim of Vacaspati, remarks, that the character of a knowledge, whether it is of a definite form (*niścayākāra*) or of an indefinite form, does not make it valid or invalid. What matters actually is non-contradiction, the possibility of actually obtaining the object indicated. But it is never possible to obtain actually an object which appears to be characterised by two mutually opposite properties. That is why doubt should be considered as deviating.[45]

Later Definitions of Valid Knowledge

The Indian philosophers' effort at finding a correct definition of valid knowledge or *pramā* continues to a later period also. As we shall presently see (though very briefly), even Gaṅgeśa in his *Tattvacintāmaṇi* devotes a section to the topic. It is quite probable that Gaṅgeśa's exposition is much influenced by the criticism of Śrīharṣa, who is rather a *vaitaṇḍika*, though affiliated to the Advaita school of Vedānta, and very much adept in demolishing the positions of others.

Śrīharṣa, in his *khaṇḍanakhaṇḍakhādya*,[46] takes up one by one no less than eight definitions of valid knowledge current among the different schools and subjects them to rigorous criticism and finally rejects them all. Obviously, we do not have the scope here to go into the elaborate polemics of Śrīharṣa in this regard, nor is it necessary for us. Still, as a specimen we may mention a few words.

Thus, for example, one of the definitions of valid knowledge as offered by some is *yathārthānubhavatva*[47]. In this definition, *yathā* implies similarity and *artha* stands for an actual object. But the question is: can there be similarity between knowledge and an object? Two things are said to be similar only when they share the same property or properties. But is there any property which can be considered as common between knowledge and an actual object? It is, in fact, next to impossible to find out such a common property.

Moreover, what is the nature of similarity-is it total or partial? The first alternative is simply absurd, because such similarity between knowledge and an object is never possible. In that case, it would not be possible to accept even a single cognition as valid. If, on the other hand, it is claimed that the similarity may be partial, one would be at liberty to establish similarity on the basis of some property whatever it may be. But, in that case, the definition would unduly apply to an invalid knowledge also. There are definitely some properties which may be equally shared by an invalid knowledge and an object, for example *prameyatva*, *sattā* etc.

While concluding his discussion on the definition of valid knowledge, Śrīharṣa hints at a common objection that may be raised against all the suggested definitions.[48] The sole purpose of valid knowledge is to produce a correct behavior towards an object. But, it may be asked, is it necessary to know beforehand some definition of *pramā* to have a correct behavior towards an object, or is it enough that there exists some definition of validity whether we know it or not? Again, if the knowledge of the definition of validity is necessary, is it not further necessary to know that the knowledge of the definition itself is valid? But the fact is that even an illiterate man can appropriately activate himself without a prior knowledge of any definition of validity. Then what is the need of defining valid knowledge at all?

If it is assumed that one is required to know the definition of valid knowledge before knowing the validity of knowledge and confidently activating oneself, then how does one know the validity of the definition itself? Is it self-determined? Then why does not the opponent admit that the validity of knowledge itself is self-determined? Otherwise the opponent will have to accept the absurd position that validity of knowledge depends on an unverified knowledge of the definition of validity.

It may be argued that it is enough that the definition exists, even though one may not be aware of it or that the knowledge of the definition exists, even though one may not be aware of its validity. But, then, what is the utility of the definition at all, if one need not know it or need not know its validity? What then will be the safeguard against taking valid knowledge as invalid and the invalid as valid? Moreover, if the opponent sticks to the point that it is enough that the definition of validity is valid 'in fact' (*vastutaḥ*), that any further determination of that validity is unwanted, then, on the same ground, one may equally argue that the definition is invalid 'in fact'.

Śrīharṣa's implication is that the opponent will be compelled to accept the principle of self-validation. People in common practice spontaneously take their knowledge to be valid as long as a contradiction does not arise.

In the *Tattvacintāmaṇi*, Gaṅgeśa also discusses a good number of definitions of valid knowledge.[49] Though some of the definitions are quite similar to one another, with not much variation still he has tried to present a list of definitions as exhaustive as possible. He has noted all the definitions current in his time and has also examined a number of definitions based on the concept of *viṣayata*. Following the usual procedure he has divided the section on the definition of valid knowledge into two parts, the position of the opponent (*pūrvapakṣa*) and the conclusion of his own (*siddhāntapakṣa*).[50] We may try to have here just a brief idea of Gaṅgeśa's critical analysis.

For example, an easy and popular definition of valid knowledge, may be formulated and valid knowledge is that which possesses validity or *pramātva*. As against this, it is asked, what is the exact nature of *pramātva*, is it a universal (*jāti*)?[51] According to some, the property should be considered a universal, because in that case there will be simplicity or parsimony (*lāghava*). Thus is can be defined as an universal which is located in valid knowledge other than the indeterminate (*nirvikalpaka*). Like the property of *abhāvatva*, it is also determined by its relatum (*pratiyogin*). Just as *ghaṭābhāvatva* is determined by its counterpositive (i.e. *ghaṭa*), so also in the case of the valid knowledge of silver in silver, *pramātva* is determined by *rajatatva* or silverness.

Now, it may be asked, *abhāvatva* is admitted to be different in each case as determined by its different counterpositives; but what is the case with *pramātva*? Should it be considered different in different cases as determined by different properties? Or, should it be accepted as one and the same in all the cases in spite of the different determinants, as is the case with *samavāya* which though having various relata is considered to be the same always?

In answer, it is said that *pramātva* is to be admitted as one and the same always to avoid manifoldness of assumptions (*kalpanāgaurava*). Moreover, if *pramātva* is admitted to be different with reference to the difference of the relatum, there will result be fallacy of intermixture (*sāṅkarya*). For example, validity as determined by silverness is present only in the awareness of silver in silver and validity as determined by potness is present only in the awareness of pot in pot. Thus they are mutually exclusive. But when one has a single awareness having as its object both silver and a pot, we find that both the said forms of validity co-exist with each other in the awareness.

In short, *pramātva* is a universal and it is one and the same in every case; a valid knowledge is an awareness which is characterised by this universal property.

Gaṅgeśa however points out a number of objections against this view.[52] There is a general rule to the effect that a universal which is located in a perceptible thing is itself perceptible, e.g. cowness, potness, etc. If *pramātva* be a universal, it should be perceptible, because it is located in *pramā* which is a perceptible thing. Thus, whenever a *pramā* is perceptually known, the universal *pramātva* as present in it also should be perceived. But if such a position is accepted there will be no logical explanation for the fact of doubt regarding the validity of a knowledge. Sometimes even though one may acquire a valid knowledge really, one may afterwards have a doubt whether the knowledge is valid or not. But if *pramātva* as present in it is already ascertained, how can there be any such doubt?

As against the above, it may be pointed out that this argument applies to all cases of doubt and as a result any form of doubt would become an impossibility. For example, when in a tree standing far away in the middle of the field one has a doubt - is it a man or a tree - one perceives the tree and also the universal tree–ness as present in it, according to the rule stated above. If tree-ness is perceptually known, how can there be a doubt? It may be answered that even though the tree is perceived at that time, tree–ness is not known perceptually, because this property remains under cover due to defect (*doṣa*). As a result, one cannot identify the object with certainty. The opponent retorts that the same argument may be applied to the case of *pramātva* also. It may be said that when one has the awareness of a valid knowledge as qualified by *pramātva* one does not have the knowledge of *pramātva* because it remains covered due to some defect. Thus even if *pramātva* be a universal, there can be produced a doubt regarding the validity of a knowledge.

Apprehending this kind of defence, Gaṅgeśa gives another argument to show that *pramātva* cannot be considered a universal. One may have a doubt in a distant object – is it a man or a tree? Afterwards, when one perceives in it some specific characteristics of one object, the doubt is dispelled. Thus, one has a perceptual knowledge in the form 'this object has things like branches etc. which are pervaded by tree-ness' and then, the definite perceptual knowledge in the form 'this is a tree'. It is to be specially noted that this final knowledge is *perceptual* in nature. But what happens in the case of a doubt regarding the validity or *pramātva* of a knowledge? After having such a doubt one actually determines its validity with the help of an awareness in the form 'this knowledge is characterised by the capability of producing a successful activity, which is pervaded by *pramātva'*. But here the final awareness or the definite cognition of validity is *inferential* in character, and not perceptual. This difference in the nature of the cognitions in the two cases indicates that the properties are different in each case. In other words, since *pramātva* is always an object of inference it cannot be accepted as a universal.

Of course, it may be asked, how is it determined that the final knowledge dispelling the doubt in the former case (i.e. this is a tree) is perceptual in nature, but the final knowledge determining the validity of knowledge is inferential in nature? It may as well be argued that the final conclusion in the form 'this knowledge is *pramā* or valid' may well be considered as a piece of perceptual knowledge. To this, it is answered that the nature of a piece of knowledge is determined by the form of the after–knowledge (*anuvyavasāya*) revealing it. Thus, after arriving at the ascertainment 'this is a tree' one has the after-knowledge in the specific form 'I *perceive* tree–ness in the object', but after ascertaining that a piece of knowledge is valid, one has the after-knowledge in the specific form 'I *infer* validity in the knowledge'. As a result, one piece of knowledge becomes perceptual and the other inferential.

Even then, the opponent of Gaṅgeśa may contend that he has no faith in such after-knowledge. An after-knowledge cannot necessarily determine the nature of a knowledge. Apprehending such a contention, Gaṅgeśa therefore advances one further argument against the opponent. The objection is based upon the fault known as the intermixture (*saṃkara*) of universals.[53]

According to the older school of Nyāya, common properties which are found to be subject to intermixture should not be accepted as universals. Intermixture means the co-existence of two such properties in a common locus as are also present in the same locus with their absolute absence. In short, in the case of intermixture two supposedly universal properties not only exist in a common locus, but each also exist in a locus along with the absence of the other, i.e. the one goes both with and without the other. *Pramātva* is vitiated by this fault of intermixture with properties like perceptual immediacy (*sākṣāttva*). Perceptual immediacy is present in all perceptual congnitions, irrespective of their validity and invalidity. In the case of an invalid perception there is perceptual immediacy, but no validity. Again, in the case of a correct inference, there is validity, but no perceptual immediacy. However, in the case of a valid perceptual knowledge, both validity and perceptual immediacy are present together.

It may be objected that the fault of intermixture occurs only in the case of properties located in substances (*dravya*) and not in the case of properties located in qualities (*guṇa*).[54] Thus validity and perceptual immediacy are properties which belong to knowledge, which again is a quality of the self. Since these do not directly belong to any substance they cannot be rejected as universal on the ground of intermixture. This is answered by pointing out that the root of the fault is the same in all the cases and hence, there is no decisive ground to indicate that in one case it is vitiating but in the other it is not so. It is a vitiating factor in all the cases equally. In short, *pramātva* cannot in any way be accepted as a universal.

Valid Knowledge in Vaiśeṣika Works

No detailed examination of the nature of valid knowledge in general is found in Vaiśeṣika literature. There is no reference to any general definition as such, although the classification is given and the various forms are discussed in details.

In Vaiśeṣika literature, the terms for valid and invalid knowledge are respectively *vidyā* and *avidyā*. This is clear from Kaṇāda's use of the words on more than one occassion. For example, in the second chapter of the *Vaiśeṣikasūtra* (VS) he says that doubt arises from *vidyā* and *avidyā*, which, according to commentators, stand for valid and invalid cognition respectively.[55]

However, at the end of the ninth chapter of the VS there is some brief discussion on the nature of these two kinds of knowledge.[56] Thus, Kaṇāda says that invalid knowledge is produced due to the defect of the sense organs and the defect of impression (*saṃskāra*). The first signifies the incapability of a sense organ to produce right knowledge because of factors like diseases, distance etc. If a person is suffering from jaundice, he perceives the white conch–shell as yellow. The size of the moon appears to be small due to very long distance. The latter defect means the absence of the awareness of a distinguishing characteristic. When one perceives one thing as another, one perceives its similarity with the other, but fails to ascertain the specific characteristic of the actual thing.

This is how, one of the commentators, Śaṅkara Miśra, explains the implications of Kaṇāda. According to him, Kaṇāda here specifies the cause of only one form of invalid knowledge, namely, error (*viparyaya*), because the causes of the other forms like dream (*svapna*) etc. have been discussed in preceding *sūtras*. But other commentators like

Candrānanda[57] and others think that actually here the causes of invalid knowledge in general have been mentioned. Thus, Candrānanda explains that in the well known case of error-when one cognises the shell as silver – the awareness is produced through a sense organ which is made incapable by imperfections like *vāta* etc., accompanied by the causes like an impression produced by the previous perception of silver, contact between the self and the mind and also a specific from of *adharma*. Then he adds that all this is true of also another form of invalid knowledge, such as indefinite knowledge (*anadhyavasāya*), which occurs, for example, when a person from the south cannot identify a camel standing before him.

According to Śaṅkara Miśra, the general definition of invalid knowledge is given by Kaṇāda in the next *sūtra* where he remakes, after a brief discussion of the different forms of invalid knowledge, such knowledge is imperfect (*duṣṭa*).[58] Of course, it is clear that the *sūtras* are cryptic and not much is available from them. There is no early commentary and it is difficult to be certain about their implications. Later commentators like Śaṅkara Miśra and adopt Navyanyāya terminology and bring into them concepts developed much later while trying to bring out the significance.[59] Thus, for example, Śaṅkara explains that imperfect knowledge means knowledge which is deviating, an awareness of *that* which is actually *not that*. Finally he defines it in later terminology as knowledge which has an incompatible property (*vyadhikaraṇa*) as its qualifier (*prakāra*), i.e. knowledge which has as its qualifier a property which is not present in the qualificand (*viśeṣya*). For example, when one wrongly perceives the shell as 'this is silver,' the property of silverness is incompatible with the shell. In other words, in this cognition the qualificand is really the shell and the qualifier is silverness. But the property is never actually present in the qualificand.

We have already referred to the controversy whether doubt is to be regarded as deviating or non-deviating. Though brief, Śaṅkara definitely considers doubt to be deviating and also gives the reason for his conclusion. He says that lack of definiteness also is an imperfection in the case of knowledge. Thus even if in the case of certain doubts one of the alternatives may be true they cannot be considered valid knowledge as they do not have definiteness.[60]

Praśastapāda also speaks of two broad classes of knowledge, namely, *vidyā* and *avidyā*. Each of them again is divided in to four forms. We shall discuss them in the subsequent chapters. Praśastapāda also does not give any general definition of valid or invalid knowledge. The commentators also do not give much information on the point. They remain content with brief remarks only.

According to the *Vyomavatī*,[61] valid knowledge means a definite ascertainment which is not contradicted in spite of the differences of space (*deśa*), time (*kāla*) and state (*avasthā*). Invalid knowledge is just opposite in nature. It is further pointed out that *vidyā* and *avidyā* should not be identified with *pramāṇa* and *apramāṇa* respectively, because it will lead to undesireable consequences. For example, if the term *pramāṇa* is analysed as 'that by which one acquires valid knowledge', even doubt (*saṃśaya*) which is considered to be a form of invalid knowledge would become *vidyā*. Right knowledge of a category cannot be acquired without doubt. When one tries to determine the nature of a category correctly, generally one has first a doubt involving alternatives. Subsequently, a critical examination is made, one of the alternatives only is found to be justified and it is accepted as the right conclusion. This is particularly true, for example, in the case of the true knowledge of the self. In other words, doubt also is instrument in producing valid knowledge (at least in some cases) and hence should be considered *vidyā*.

Moreover, in some cases a valid knowledge may actually produce another valid knowledge and play the role of *pramāṇa*. But this is not true of all the cases of valid knowledge. Thus the definition would be narrow as it will not apply to such cases.

It may be claimed that the term *pramāṇa* does not mean the instrument of valid knowledge but rather the result obtained by the operation of an instrument of valid knowledge. In that case the definition would not apply to the doubt etc. because they are not produced by a *pramāṇa*. But this is also not satisfactory. According to Praśastapāda, recollection (*smṛti*) is a form of valid knowledge, but the source of recollection is not accepted as a *pramāṇa*. The Vaiśeṣikas accept only two *pramāṇas*, perception and inference, and if the source of recollection is given the status of a *pramāṇa*, it will mean accepting third and as such, will go against their accepted position.

The commentary also refers to another definition offered by others. According to it, *vidyā* means knowledge (*vijñāna*) which is the cause of a specific activity (*viśiṣṭa-vyavahāra*), and *avidyā* is the opposite. However, this view does not find favour with the commentator. What exactly is the meaning of specific activity? If it is taken to mean an activity for obtaining an object (*pravṛtti*) or an activity for avoiding an object (*nivṛtti*), the definition would apply even to doubt etc. A doubt regarding the nature of an object also may induce one either to collect an object or to avoid an object.

It may be suggested that a specific activity means a cognition in the form 'I have rightly known in spite of the differences of space etc'. But this also will make the definition narrow, because it will not be applicable to all forms of *vidyā*. It is not that we have such a form of knowledge or specific activity in the case of each and every form of *vidyā*.

In the *Nyāyakandalī*[62] we have a brief comment only mentioning the essential characteristics of valid knowledge, which are all more or less accepted by the different schools of Indian philosophy. Thus *vidyā* means an awareness which is free from doubt, not contradicted and of the nature of a definite assertion. We have already discussed the implications of these. According to the commentators of Śrīdhara, the first two characteristics exclude respectively doubt and error, and the third is mentioned for the purpose of excluding indefinite knowledge which according to the Vaiśeṣikas is a special form of *avidyā* as distinct from doubt. There is no further discussion and they do not go into such questions as whether the exclusion of doubt also is possible or not by the third characteristic, etc.

According to Udayana,[63] *vidyā* means the knowledge of an object as it really is or valid knowledge (*yathārtha jñāna*). Though he himself does not elaborate the definition, his commentator Vardhamāna discusses it in some details.[64] However, as we shall presently see, he does not offer anything new, but only adopts a later terminology and collects some information which are already treated in the *Tattvacintāmaṇi*.

Thus, for example, following the generally accepted view, he comments that if *vidyā* is simply defined as valid knowledge (*jñāna*) it would be applicable also to recollection, because it is a form of knowledge and is valid when the basic cognition generating it is valid. The difficulty may be avoided by modifying the definition to the effect that *vidyā* is valid awareness (*anubhava*). Traditionally, knowledge is first divided into two classes, namely, recollection or representative and awareness or presentative. Thus recollection will automatically be excluded from the category of *vidyā*, if it is defined as awareness. But here also there will be a difficulty, because the definition will unduly apply to certain cases of doubt, i.e. doubts where one of the alternatives is true.

Next, Vardhamāna refers to a definition offered by some, namely, a valid knowledge means an ascertainment (*niścaya*) which is *yathārtha*.[65] The word *yathā* here means similarity and thus the implication would be that when there is similarity between the object and the knowledge, the awareness can be accepted as valid. But the question is, what is the point of similarity between the two? Is it implied that the object and the knowledge should be totally similar? Obviously the answer cannot be in the affirmative. The two can never be totally similar and thus it would be difficult to find even a single instance of valid knowledge. If, on the other hand, it is claimed that the two should share only some particular properties, then, the definition will become applicable to even invalid knowledge, because properties like *vācyatva*, *prameyatva* etc. are present in both the forms of knowledge.

Again, valid knowledge may be defined as a cognition which has as its qualifier (*prakāra*) a property located in the qualificand (*viśeṣya*) When one cognises a jar as a jar the qualifier is jarness which is actually located in the jar. But when one cognises the rope as the snake the qualifier is snake-ness, but it is not actually present in the rope. This definition is rejected on the ground that it does not apply to indeterminate (*nirvikalpaka*) knowledge, which is by definition without any qualifier.

The difficulty can be avoided by a slight modification of the definition. Thus, valid knowledge may be defined as a cognition which does not have as qualifier a property which is not located in the qualificand. Since indeterminate knowledge is devoid of any qualifier the definition will apply to it. However, there are other difficulties involved in this definition.[66]

For example, the definition requires that the qualifier should be such a property as is not located in the qualificand. Does it mean that the qualifying property should not be a property located in *some* instances of qualificand? In that case, it would not be applicable to the valid *samūhālambana* cognition in the form 'these are a jar and a cloth'. In this cognition, one of the qualifiers is *ghaṭatva*, but it is not present in one of the qualificands, namely, cloth. Similarly, *paṭatva* the other qualifier is not present in a jar, which is one of the qualificands.

Of course, it may be pointed out that in the above example there are two qualificands, namely, a jar and a cloth and also, two qualifiers, namely *ghaṭatva* and *paṭatva*. Since *ghaṭatva* is present in the jar and *paṭatva* in the cloth, we cannot really say that the qualifiers are not present in all the qualificands. In other words, it is implied that a cognition will be invalid only if the qualifier is found to be not present in *all* the qualificands.

But this defence also is not considered satisfactory, because then the definition will unduly apply to a case of *samūhālambana* cognition which is partially valid and partially invalid. For example, when a piece of tin and a piece of silver are lying at a distance, one may wrongly perceive both as silver and have the *samūhālambana* cognition namely, 'these two are silver'. Here one of the qualifiers is silverness and it is actually present is one of the qualificands, namely, silver. It may not be present in the other qualificand, namely, the tin but it cannot be considered as a property which is not present in all the qualificands. So this definition also is not accepted.

It may be argued that the real implication is that in the case of a valid knowledge the qualifier should be a property which is absent from all the qualificands. In the above instance, the qualifier 'silverness' is not so, because it is present in silver, one of the qualificands. Hence, the definition does not apply to it. But, in that case, the definition will not be applicable to the valid *samūhālambana* cognition is the form 'these two are jar are a cloth.' Here the two qualifiers are not present in all the qualificands, because *ghaṭatva* and *paṭatva* are respectively not present in a cloth and jar.

A lot of definitions of *pramā* is based upon the inviolability of valid knowledge. For example, according to some, valid knowledge may be defined as an awareness which is not contradicted (*abādhita*).[67] When one cognises silver as silver in the form 'this is silver' the cognition is not subsequently set aside by another cognition. But when one cognises tin as silver the cognition is later set aside by another cognition, namely, 'this is tin'. In the first case, the qualifier (silverness) is ascertained to be present in the qualificand (silver) and hence there is absence of contradiction. In the latter case, however, the qualifier is ascertained to be absent from the qualificand and hence there is contradiction. A valid knowledge must be free from such contradiction. This uncontradictedness is the essence of valid knowledge.

This definition also is found to be unsatisfactory. The notion of uncontradictedness involves the notion of contradiction. An invalid knowledge suffers form contradiction, but the question is whether the contradictory itself should be a valid knowledge or not. The contender of the definition obviously means that a valid knowledge cannot be contradicted by another valid knowledge. For example, a person may notice a piece of shell and rightly take it to be so. Sometimes later the same person very much occupied with the thought of getting a piece of silver may find the same shell and take it to be silver. The second knowledge stands in contradiction to the first knowledge, but it is a false contradictory. So the contender's notion of uncontradictedness is bound to depend on a presupposed notion of a *valid* contradictory which in its turn involves the notion of validity which is yet to be defined. Thus the definition suffers from the fault of self-dependence. Or, it may be treated as a case of mutual dependence. The notion of validity depends on the notion of uncontradictedness and *vice versa.*

The whole of the discussion on the different definitions of *pramā* offered by others, which are ultimately rejected, is based upon Gaṅgeśa's examination of such definitions. Of course, Vardhamāna has been rather selective and has chosen to refer to just a few definitions, while Gaṅgeś a's examination is thorough and he has discussed many other definitions based upon various aspects and concepts, involving a lot of Navyanyāya terminology. Vardhamāna has quoted from Gaṅgeśa almost verbatim, but he has never mentioned his name. His references to the definitions and the grounds for their rejection are also very brief and cryptic.

The same is true so far as Vardhamāna's reference to a correct or acceptable definition of valid knowledge is concerned. Here also he quotes from Gaṅgeśa and confines his discussion to some brief remarks only.[68] Thus, the conclusive definition of *pramā* is said to be an awareness of a property (or, a thing) in a locus in which it is actually present. In other words, a cognition is false if the qualifier does not occur in, or is not contained in, the qualificand; otherwise it is true. Of course, it may be objected that the definition does not apply to indeterminate knowledge, since it is not a qualificative cognition. The definition is designed to apply to determinate knowledge only. The difficulty is easily avoided by pointing out that it is not intended to apply to indeterminate knowledge. In fact, it has been argued that indeterminate knowledge can be determined neither as valid nor as invalid. The definition can be easily illustrated by the cognition of silver in silver or the cognition of silver in shell.

Some objections against this definition also have been raised and answers have been given.[69] For example, in a shell lying before him, a person has the cognition 'this is silver'. Actually, it is a case of invalid knowledge. Here the qualificand (shell) is not characterised by the qualifier (silverness). But it may be argued that here we can also take as qualificand and qualifier respectively the thing referred to as 'this' and the property of thisness. In that case, however the cognition should be treated as valid. Therefore, what would be the actual nature of the cognition? Should it be treated as valid or invalid?

In answer, Gaṅgeśa points out that in such a case there is no difficulty because actually there is no opposition. There is opposition between a valid knowledge having this-ness as qualifier and an invalid knowledge having this-ness as qualifier. But there is no opposition between a valid cognition having this–ness as qualifier and an invalid cognition having silverness as qualifier. In other words, the awareness 'this is silver' in shell may be considered both as valid and invalid. So far as the qualificand part is concerned it is valid, but with reference to the qualifier part it is invalid.

It has been further contended that there will be difficulty in the case of a cognition involving a property or thing which has non-pervasive occurrence (*avyāpyavṛtti*). For example, the cognition 'the tree has conjunction with monkey' should be treated as both valid and invalid. The conjunction is present in the tree only in a particular portion (branches), but it is absent from some particular portions (root etc.). With reference to the branches the cognition should be valid, but with reference to the root it should be invalid. Similarly, the cognition 'the tree has absence of conjunction with monkey' should also be considered as sharing the double characteristics.

While answering the objection, Gaṅgeśa first refers to the view of Vallabhācārya. According to him, conjunction also has pervasive occurrence. Thus, when the monkey is actually sitting on a branch of the tree, conjunction with monkey is present in the whole of the tree and there can be no absence of such conjunction in the tree. Hence the objection pointed out above has no scope. Gaṅgeśa however does not accept this view. According to him, both conjunction with monkey and absence of conjunction with monkey have non-pervasive occurrence. While considering the presence or absence of a property or a thing in the locus we have to take into consideration also the delimiting part (*avaccheda*). Thus, if the cognition of conjunction with monkey refers to a branch it should be considered as a case of valid knowledge only; if it refers to the root it should be considered as a case of invalid knowledge only. The same principle should be applied to determine the character of the cognition 'the tree has absence of conjunction with monkey'.[70]

NOTES & REFERENCES

1. VS 1.1.4.
2. NS 1.1.3.
3. Potter, Encyclopedia of Indian Philosophies, vol. II p. 282.
4. See, for example, MM, verse 2.
5. Cf. Vācaspati's discussion of Mīmāṃsā view, NVTT, p. 35.

6. Ibid. for a good exposition of the view, see Bagchi, Prācīna Nyāya O Prācīna Mīmāṃsā Darśana Sammata Prāmānyavāda.
7. NM, pt. I, P. 21.
8. NVTT, on NS 1.1.4, p. 238.
9. Sukhlalji Sanghvi, Advanced studies in Indian logic & Metaphysics, p. 50.
10. See, for example, NKu, verse 4.1.
11. MM, p.3.
12. VP, Ch. I.
13. NVTT, p. 35.
14. NM, pp.21f.
15. NVTT, p.21 and NM, ibid.
16. PP, pp.42-43.
17. NBT, p.6.
18. HBT, p.37.
19. TSV, 1.10.28, 1.13.94, 1.13.15 and PKM, p.16.
20. NVTT, on NS 1.1.1., p.24.
21. Ibid.
22. On NS 1.1.3.
23. NV, p.9.
24. NVTT, p.35.
25. MM, p.4.
26. MM, pt. I, p.12, Jayanta's general definition of *pramāṇa*.
27. ON SK, verse 4.
28. See, for example, *Pūrṇimā* commentary by Pancānana Tarkaratna on SK verse 4.
29. On NS 1.1.4, translation by Chattopadhyaya and Gangopadhyaya.
30. Ibid.
31. Ibid.
32. NVTT, p.224.
33. Ibid, p.225.
34. Ibid, cf. *Pariśuddhi* also, p.268.
35. Ibid, pp.225-226.

36. Phaṇibhūṣaṇa Tarkavāgiśa, Nyāyadarśana, vol.1, pp. 136f.
37. NVTT, p.226.
38. PM, p.36.
39. NM, pt. I, p. 84.
40. Ibid, p.85.
41. See, Phaṇibhūṣaṇa Tarkavāgiśa, *Nyāyadarśana*, vol.1, p.131.
42. *Pariśuddhi* on NS 1.1.4, p.268.
43. Ibid.
44. Ibid.
45. Ibid.
46. KKK, p. 130ff.
47. Ibid, p 218. This is Udayana's definition; NKu 4.1. See also TCM, p.381.
48. Ibid, p.239.
49. TCM, p.372.
50. Ibid, p.401.
51. Ibid, p. 372 f. The explanation given is acccording to Mathurānātha's commentary.
52. Ibid. Here also the implications have been explained following Mathurānātha.
53. The list of *jāti–bādhakas* is given by Udayana in the *Kiraṇāvalī* while explaining *sāmānya*. *Saṃkara* is the third one. According to some, however, it is not a *jāti-bādhaka*.
54. Mathurānātha, p.374.
55. VS 2.2.20.
56. VS 9.2.10-12
57. VS (C) pp.70-71.
58. VS 9.2.12.
59. On ibid.
60. On VS 9.2.11.
61. pp. 115-116.
62. p.414.
63. *Kiraṇāvalī*, p.512.
64. Ibid, pp.512-513.

65. TCM, p.381.

66. Ibid, p.386f.

67. Ibid, p. 382.

68. *Prakāśa*, p.512 and TCM, p.401.

69. TCM, pp.401 f. and Mathurānātha's commentary thereon.

70. Ibid., pp. 409 f. and Mathurānātha's commentary thereon.

Chapter Two

Perception

Perception in The Vaiśeṣikasūtra

As we have already pointed out, the VS is not a systematic work. The topics are scattered all over the text and are often mentioned in connection with some other problem which is actually the main topic. This is true of the sources of knowledge also. They have not been discussed following a definite plan. It is well known that the Vaiśeṣika accepts only two sources of knowledge, perception and inference. But no where in the VS the fact is implicitly or explicitly mentioned. Moreover, the comments are sometimes very brief.

As regards perception also, we have too little in the VS. Perception as such is not discussed on any occasion. But we have definite references to perception or the cause of perception on a few occasions. Thus, we have such references in various contexts-in the context of showing how the self is to be inferred, in the context of proving that the mind as an instrument of knowledge has to be admitted and in the context of proving that the mind can be characterised by movement.[1]

Whatever may be the context, one point is clear enough, namely, perception is a form of knowledge produced from contacts (*sannikarṣa*) among the four, i.e. self, mind, sense organ and object.[2] As later commentators state, perception occurs when the self comes in contact with the mind, the mind comes in contact with the sense organ and finally, the sense organ comes in contact with the object. Commentators like Śaṅkara Miśra and others who are much later and under the influence of theories developed much later try to read into these cryptic *sūtras* various implications, though it is doubtful how far such interpretation can be justified logically and historically. We shall briefly refer to it later.

On the other hand, we can have some interesting information in this connection from Buddhist sources. In the first chapter of the *Pramāṇasamuccaya* which deals with perception, Diṅnāga has critically discussed the Vaiśeṣika view of perception. In the autocommentary (*vṛtti*) he actually quotes one *sūtra* of Kaṇāda. He makes an interesting comment about the actual instrument of perception in the Vaiśeṣika view. He says that unlike the Buddhists some philosophers admit that *pramāṇa* and its effects are different and moreover, some of them think that the sense-object contact is the actual instrument while others think that the self-mind contact is the actual instrument.[3]

Jinendrabuddhi clarifies the comment of Diṅnāga. According to him, the first alternative, is the view of Śrayaska and others. They think that in the case of perception the sense-object contact is the special cause (*asādhāraṇa*) and the other contacts, though necessary, are common (*sādhāraṇa*) to other forms of knowledge also, such as memory etc. The second alternative is put forward by Ravana and others. They argue that the self-mind contact should be the instrument of perception, because the self and the mind are the principal (*pradhāna*) factors. The self is considered more important than the others because it is the agent who acquires knowledge, it is a substance inferred on the basis of knowledge and finally it experiences the results. The mind also is more important than the others, because it apprehends all kind of objects and is necessary for the production of any form of knowledge.[4]

The above becomes further interesting if we consider the discussion made by Gautama in the section on the critical examination (*parīkṣā*) of perception in the second chapter of the NS. Earlier, in the first chapter, while explaining the definition of perception as given by Gautama, Vātsyāyana also hints at the controversy.[5] Gautama defines perception by referring to its cause. But, then, he should also mention the contact between the self and the mind, because there can be no perception in the absence of such a contact also. Vātsyāyana replies that Gautama has mentioned only the special or uncommon cause of perception, because that only is necessary for a proper definition of perception, his purpose here is not to enumerate all the causes of perception. So he has left out the common cause.

However, the discussion of Gautama himself is more elaborate and the point. The view that the self-mind contact is the instrument in the case of perception is presented by Gautama as the opponent's contention. He discusses the view but finally gives his own conclusion by maintaining that the sense-object contact is the instrument.

The objection against Gautama's definition of perception is that it is incomplete, because one of the causes of perception, the self-mind contact, has not been mentioned.[6] It is a fact that just as there can be no perception in the absence of sense-object contact, so also there can be no perception in the absence of contact between the self and the mind. Vātsyāyana explains the objection :

"The quality resulting from conjunction cannot be produced in a substance which is not conjoined. The contact of the mind with the self is a cause of perception, because knowledge is found to be produced in the self from it. The contact of the mind with the sense-organ is also a cause of perception, because, if the sense-object contact is accepted as the cause of perception independent of the contact with the mind, then cognitions will arise simultaneously."[7]

Moreover, the claim that sense-object contact should be the instrument of perception because perceptual knowledge is found to be immediately preceded by it, is not justified. In that case, one would have to accept as the cause of perception contacts with time, space and *ākāśa* also. They are eternal and all-pervasive substances and contacts with them are unavoidable.[8]

Refuting the opponent, Gautama first says that though self-mind contact has not been included in the definition its role is in no way denied. Gautama has categorically stated that knowledge is a mark for the inference of the self as a distinct entity. It implies that knowledge inheres in the self and the self is a cause of all forms of knowledge. In fact, self-mind contact is regarded as the cause of all forms of knowledge including perception.[9]

Gautama continues by explaining why sense-object contact alone has been mentioned in so many words. Gautama mentions only the distinguishing cause of perceptual knowledge. Though the self-mind contact and the mind-sense contact are both causes of perception, they are not mentioned in the definition, because the mention of the former makes the definition too wide and the mention of the latter makes it too narrow. The former is necessary for not only perception but also for other forms of knowledge, while the latter is not present in the case of internal perception.[10]

Gautama further mentions two typical examples which show that compared to the contact of the self with mind sense-object contact is primary. A person goes to sleep after resolving to wake up at a particular time and he actually wakes up at that time because of his resolution. By contrast, a person who goes to sleep without any such resolution, may suddenly wake up because of a loud sound or a violent push. Primary cause of the knowledge that wakes him up is the sense-object contact and not any conscious guidance of his mind by the self. Here we clearly see that sense-object contact is primary and self-mind contact is secondary in producing the perceptual knowledge. The same is found in the case of an inattentive person who perceives an object suddenly presented before him. A person may have his mind preoccupied with something else and may not be desirous of having the knowledge of a particular object. But that particular object is suddenly thrust upon him and he is compelled to have an awareness of it. In this case the role of sense-object contact is primary and that of self-mind contact secondary, because he is not guiding his mind through motivation with the intention of having the knowledge of the particular object.[11]

According to Gautama another ground for the primacy of sense-object contact is the fact that perceptions are named by the senses and their objects. A person after acquiring some knowledge says 'I smell with the olfactory sense' or 'I have an olfactory perception,' or I have a smell-perception', and so on. Five forms of perception are spoken of as there are five external senses and their respective objects. Thus usage also indicates that in perception sense-object contact is primary.[12]

It has been shown that in the case of a person sleeping without any resolution or an inattentive person the primary cause of perceptual knowledge is the sense–object contact. Contacts of the self with the mind and of the mind with the senses are also present there, but they do not actively contribute to the knowledge. What then activates the mind to come in contact with the self and the senses in such cases? In answer, Vātsyāyana says that it is *adṛṣṭa*. In the case of a person awake or attentive, the mind is activated by motivation which results in his self from the desire to know such an object. Such a desire being absent in the case of a person asleep or inattentive, it must be admitted that there is some other quality to activate the mind to come in contact with the self and the objects. This quality is *adṛṣṭa* which is the universal cause of everything and is itself the result of good and bad actions and evils like attachment etc.[13]

In short, it is possible that at least in the earliest phase the Vaiśeṣika and the Nyāya follow different traditions in the treatment of perception.

Conditions of Perceptibility

Besides some brief remarks about how perception is produced, we have in the VS also some discussion about the conditions of perceptibility.

Referring to the perceptibility of a substance (*dravya*), the VS says that to be perceptible a substance should have large magnitude (*mahattva*), should be composed of many parts (*anekadravyavattva*) and should have colour (*rūpa*).[14] Thus, because of the absence of large magnitude an atom is not perceived. Air is not perceived due to the absence of colour. Śaṅkara Miśra has discussed the question whether both of the first two conditions and necessary or not. According to some, the presence of large magnitude is enough, and the mention of being composed of many parts is not necessary, because whatever is of a large magnitude is also composed of many parts. But the commentator argues that both the conditions are equally necessary. For example, when at a distance a small club (*mudgara*) is placed on a large piece of cloth made of fine yarns, the club is perceived and the cloth is not, although there is excellence of large magnitude in the latter. This indicates that perceptibility may also depend on excellence with reference to the number of component parts.[15]

Again, referring to the conditions which make the quality of colour perceptible through the visual sense, it said that the perception of colour is due to its inherence in a substance made of many parts and the presence of a specific property in the colour. According to the commentator, the specific properties which are to be present in the colour are three, namely, being manifest (*udbhūtatva*), being not latent (*anudbhūtatva*) and *rūpatva*. The colour of an atom is not perceived, because it is not present in a substance made of many parts. The quality of touch is not visually known because of the absence of *rūpatva* in it. The rays of the visual sense or their colour are not perceived because the colour present in them is not manifest.[16]

It is interesting to note that exactly the same *sūtra* is found in Gautama's work also.[17] According to Vātsyāyana, this specific property of colour means only property of being manifest. Vātsyāyana also gives a number of illustrations. Thus, the visual rays are not perceived as they have latent colour. The same element of fire is found to have different characteristics. It may sometimes be visible with manifest colour and manifest touch, as in the case of the rays of the sun. It may be visible with manifest colour but latent touch, as in the case of the rays of a lamp. It may also be invisible with manifest touch but latent colour when it is mixed up with water etc. It may be invisible with latent colour and latent touch, as in the case of visual rays.

The same conditions are to be adopted with the necessary

variations in the case of the perception of other three qualities, namely, taste (*rasa*), smell (*gandha*) and touch (*sparśa*). Thus the conditions for the perceptibility of taste through an external sense are being manifest, being not latent and *rasatva*. Presence in a substance made of many parts is also to be added as a general condition. Thus, smell of the olfactory sense is not perceived because it is not manifest and the smell of a stone is not so because it is latent there. The commentator has given some typical examples. In hot water, the bright white colour of fire is latent and the cold touch of water is subdued. Hence they are not perceived. In the case of gold, the colour is manifest, but its specific properties, namely, whiteness and brightness are subdued by the yellow colour of the earth–element mixed up with it. Hence its actual colour is not perceived.[18]

As regards the perception of the categories of quality and action as well as universal, the general condition is briefly stated. They are perceived if they are present in a perceptible substance, when the particular substance comes in contact with the sense. This is because they cannot be directly connected with the sense, the connection with the sense always occurs through their substratum which is the substance.[19]

There is at least one *sūtra* in the VS which refers to the perception of the self. Of course, it is an internal perception and it is said to result from a particular conjunction between the self and the mind. Śaṅkara Miśra thinks that such perception of the self is really possible for the yogins only, and very rarely in the case of an ordinary person, though, again, being subdued by ignorance, it is as good as non-existent. Moreover, the speciality of the conjunction between the self and the mind here consists in its being assisted by *dharma* produced by the practice of *yoga*.[20]

Praśastapāda's Definition of Perception

In the first instance, Praśastapāda offers a simple definition of perception based on the grammatical analysis of the term *pratyakṣa*.[21] Perception is that form of right knowledge which is produced when there is a contact with the sense. The senses are clearly enumerated and they include both the external and the internal ones. The external five are the olfactory, the gustatory, the visual, the tactual and the auditory, and the internal one is the mind.

But this simple definition also unduly applies to doubt, because it is also produced through a contact with sense. The author of *Vyomavatī* says that the difficulty does not arise, because perception is actually a form of right knowledge and the essential characteristic of a right knowledge should be shared by it. A doubt is a form of invalid knowledge and does not share that characteristic. Hence the definition does not apply to it.

He further notes that other adopt a different means. According to them, the term *vyavasāyātmaka* (of a definite character) which occurs in the definition of perception as offered in an allied system (*samāna-tantra*)[22] may be borrowed and added to the present definition. It will easily exclude doubt from the scope of perception.

In one of his later remarks Praśastapāda points to some characteristics of perception. One of them is referred to by the term *avyapadeśya*, not due to words. According to the *Vyomavatī*, that term also is to be added to the general definition of perception. In some cases, a knowledge may be produced through the instrumentality of both the sense and the word (*śabda*). For example, the visual sense of one who does not know that the word *rūpa* denotes colour may come is contact with colour, but then one does not have a knowledge identifying the thing specifically as colour. But if the sense–object contact is there and also a statement to the effect that it is colour, one acquires a knowledge in the form 'it is colour'. This is not a proper case of perception and to exclude, such knowledge the expression 'not due to words' is to be added.[23]

He also thinks thát here also the six well known sense-object contacts are available by implication. They are: conjunction (*saṃyoga*), inherence in the conjoined (*saṃyukta-samavāya*), inherence in what is inhering in the conjoined (*saṃyukta-samaveta-samavāya*), inherence (*samavāya*), inherence in the inhered (*samaveta-samavāya*) and lastly, the qualifier-qualificand relation (*viśeṣya-viśeṣaṇa-bhāva*).[24]

Śrīdharācārya points out that though here only a statement regarding the cause of perception has been made, it can also serve as a proper definition. The actual purpose of a definition is to differentiate the thing defined from things both similar and dissimilar. If an effect is described as being produced from a special or specific cause, it may very well fulfill the same purpose. For example, a barley-sprout may be defined as a thing produced from the barley-seed and since no other sprout or any thing else is produced from such a seed it may be accepted as a proper definition. Similar is the case with perception; no other form of knowledge is produced from sense-object contact.[25]

Of course, pleasure (*ṣukha*), pain (*duḥkha*) and an impression (*saṃskāra*) are also produced form such contact. But the definition of perception would not be applicable to them, because it occurs under the section on cognition (*buddhi*) in general. The implication is that perception means not only what is due to sense-object contact but also something which is of the nature of cognition.[26] According to the. Vaiśeṣika, pleasure etc. are different qualities and not, as the Buddhist contends, identical with knowledge.[27]

It is generally accepted that the instrument of perception is sense-object contact. But the definition as it stands would not agree with the view. Śrīdharācārya admits that the objection is valid, but says that the difficulty may be avoided by taking the term in the sense of the instrumental (*karaṇa*). Thus perception would mean the instrument by which such a form of knowledge is produced and it would apply to such contact. Like the author of *Vyomavatī*, he also agrees that doubt and error, though produced through such contact, are excluded from the scope of perception, because they do not represent forms of valid knowledge, and the whole discussion is being done under the general section of valid knowledge.[28]

Śrīdharācārya notes an objection which may be raised if sense–object contact is accepted as the instrument of perception. When an object comes in contact with the sense, there is also contact with its general properties and also the specific properties. Thus, just as the former would be perceived the latter also would be equally known. If it be actually so, there can never be knowledge in the form of doubt or error. When general properties only are known and there is no awareness of specific properties there can be a doubt. Similarly, if the specific properties of an object are already known, it is not possible to cognise it as something else and there would be no scope for an error.[29]

Answering the objection Śrīdharācārya says that there is no rule that both the general and the specific properties are always perceived simultaneously. The conditions for the perception of the two are not exactly the same. The general properties, as they are related to many, are perceived simply by a contact with the visual sense. But the specific properties are related to a very smaller number and their perception results when there is a contact of the visual sense and a large number of its component parts with the object which is the substratum of this specific properties and also a greater number of its component parts. As an illustrator, he says that because of this reason there is only an indistinct perception of an object at a distance, for in such a case the parts of the outgoing rays of light from the visual sense get diffused in the intervening space, and hence fail to get at the object in the proper manner.[30]

Udayana offers a different line of interpretation. He says that while dissolving the compound in the term *pratyakṣa*, Praśastapāda only refers to its etymology (*vyutpatti*) and it is not meant to supply any general definition. In fact, he does not seem to lay stress on the sense-object contact as the most important characteristic for defining perception. If perception is defined as knowledge produced from sense-object contact, it would be too wide, because it would apply to memory–knowledge, doubt, inferential knowledge of the self and others. Such forms of knowledge are produced from a contact with the internal as well as the external senses. Besides, this definition is also narrow, because it does not apply to the perception of God who is conceived to be without a body or sense organ.[31]

Udayana therefore takes into consideration another special characteristic of perception as its defining character. Perception is a form of valid knowledge which is direct or immediate (*sākṣātkāri*). What is really common to, and distinctive of, all perceptions is a feeling of directness or immediacy of the knowledge given by them. As soon as an object is presented to the sense we have an awareness about it. We say that we perceive an object if and when we know it directly, i.e. without taking the help of any previous experience or any reasoning process or the like.[32] When at mid-day one turns one's eyes overhead, one sees the sun directly, and not by means of any process of inference or reasoning. There is neither any necessity nor any time for one to think and reason before the perception of the sun arises. That it is not so in the case of knowledge derived through inference, comparison and verbal testimony is easily proved by experience and hence there is no possibility of the definition being wide.

Conditions for Perception and Its Varieties

After giving the general definition of perception, Praśastapāda points out that, of the six categories, perceptual knowledge can be produced in respect of only the first four, namely, substance, quality, action and universal. There can be no perceptual knowledge of last two categories, namely, particularity and inherence. But it is also to be noted that the conditions for perception are not the same in all cases. They differ according to the nature of the category. Even among substances the conditions vary. Since substance is the most vital category of all he specially discusses how perceptual knowledge is produced in respect of the various substances.

The conditions for perception in the case of the first three substances (earth, water, fire) are the same.[33] It is easy to see that they are more or less the same as those mentioned in the VS. First of all, to be perceptible, these substances must have the large magnitude. From the comments of the author of *Vyomavatī* and Śrīdhara it is not clear whether presence of large magnitude is a necessary condition or not, although as we have already seen the VS specifically mentions it to be so. Udayana however categorically states that presence of large magnitude is to be considered as a condition. His argument for the conclusion seems to be based on the law of concomitant variation. Excellence of perception depends upon and varies with the excellence of the large magnitude. Hence, there must be a casual connection between the two.[34]

So far as the second condition is concerned there is no disagreement. It consists in being composed of many parts. It is however interesting to note that in later Nyāya-Vaiśeṣika literature both presence of large magnitude and possession of many parts are not considered necessary for perception. Generally, the former is accepted as the cause, but the latter is rejected as *anyathāsiddha*. In fact, each of these two characteristics invariably accompanies each other. If a substance has large magnitude, it cannot but be composed of many parts; for example a dyad is not perceptible, because it is composed of only two atoms. But when three dyads combine to produce a triad, the effect becomes perceptible, because it is composed by at least three parts. On the other hand, whatever is composed of many parts cannot but be characterised by large magnitude. While enumerating the causes producing large magnitude, Kaṇāda specifically mentions that it is produced by the multiplicity of components (*karaṇa-vahutva*). In other words, every perceptible substance must have a large magnitude and would be composed of many parts. Thus, both these characteristics would be equally invariable antecedents in relation to the effect, namely, perception. It is not easy to accept one and reject the other. The later Nyāya-Vaiśeṣikas therefore take the help of the concept of *anyathāsiddha* and contend that the latter, though equally antecedent, is not a cause, because with reference to the former (which is *laghu*) it is *guru*.[35]

Of course, the concept of *anyathāsiddha* appears to be a later development. The definition of cause and its various modifications and clarifications are not available in earlier literature. Perhaps that is why the earlier authorities accept both as the cause of perception without entering into any intricate analysis following the simple principle that whatever is an invariable antecedent is a cause. However, though a much later commentator, Śaṅkara Miśra is sometimes found to support the earlier views in preference to the later ones. As we have already seen, in this case also, he has argued for accepting the latter as a cause, though on a different ground, namely, the excellence of perception varying with the excellence of the latter characteristic. We have also presently seen that Udayana uses the same argument for considering large magnitude as the cause.

The next condition, namely, presence of manifest colour is also universally accepted. A substance to be perceptible by the visual sense must have manifest colour. The possession of colour is not sufficient, the colour must have a special property, which is manifestedness. It is not enough that a substance is composed of many parts or has a large magnitude; to be perceptible it must also have such colour. For example, according to the Vaiśeṣika, the visual sense is of the nature of fire. It is composed of many parts and has a large magnitude, but due to the absence of manifest colour in it, it is not perceived.

These three conditions represent certain properties which are to be present in substances themselves. Praśastapāda adds two more conditions which may be called external ones. The first of them, namely, contacts among the four,[36] is obviously a reiteration of what we find in the VS. Just like Kaṇāda, Praśastapāda also admits that for perception contacts among the self, the mind, the sense organ and the object are essential.

But Praśastapāda differs in mentioning another condition, namely the presence of the totality of the causes like *dharma*, *adharma* and others. According to Śrīdhara, 'others' means causes like space and time and it is necessary to add the last condition, because all cognitions become causes for pleasure and pain and also because they are produced as specifically related to a particular point of space and a particular point of time. Udayana however offers a slightly different view. According to him, there are certain causes which are general to all effects, namely, *dharma*, *adharma*, space, time and God. Thus the last condition has been added to show that there general causes are also necessary in the case of perception.[37]

Śrīdhara has justified the inclusion of these different conditions with typical examples. As in the case of an atom or a dyad we have no perception, it has been stated that the substance must have a large magnitude. The variations in the large number of component parts of a substance correspondingly make the perception of a substance distinct or indistinct and that is why the presence of a large number of component part has been mentioned as a cause of perception. The substance called air has a large magnitude and is also composed of many parts, yet it is not perceived. To explain this the presence of manifested colour has been mention as a condition. He has given also another example. Fire when mixed up with water is not perceived because of the absence of this condition. Contacts among the four should obviously be a condition because perception is primarily dependent upon them.[38]

Praśastapāda states that when all these conditions are present there is produced a mere awareness (*alocanāmātra*) of the nature (*svarūpa*) of the object. All the commentators take the mere awareness in the sense of indeterminate perception (*nirvikalpaka-pratyakṣa*), and brings in the controversy whether both the forms of perception, indeterminate and determinate, are to be accepted or not.[39]

For example, Śrīdhara says that, according to some, the determinate (*savikalpaka*) should be the only form of perception. The main function of knowledge is to lead one to practical activity. But such activity is possible only when there is a determinate perception. Even animals who are devoid of any comprehension of the meanings of words turn to action only after they have determinate cognition of the object. Thus, indeterminate perception has no relevance and should not be regarded as genuine perception. This contention is refuted here by accepting the indeterminate as a form of perception.[40]

Śrīdhara argues that determinate knowledge is said to be the cause of activity, but determinate knowledge itself is not possible without the admission of a prior indeterminate knowledge. In the case of determinate knowledge, one perceives an object as qualified by the term denoting it (*vācaka-śabda*). If however there is beforehand no awareness of the nature of the object through indeterminate knowledge there can be no recollection of the denoting term and as a result, there can be no determinate knowledge either.

Śrīdhara explains further the concept of indeterminate knowledge. It cannot be said that this indeterminate knowledge presents only the generality (*sāmānya*), because its individuality (*viśeṣa*) or difference with other objects is also apprehended. It cannot also be said that it pertains to only specific particularity (*svalakṣaṇa*), because the generality is also apprehended as is clear from the fact that it is distinctly recalled on the subsequent perception of another individual of the same class. As a matter of fact, it pertains to both generality and individuality, though it is true that there is no awareness of the distinction between the two in the form 'this is generality and this is individuality.' This is due to the fact that at the time of the perception there is no perception of another object of the same class. It is only when one thing is cognised as having the same general character as another that we have a motion of generality as distinct from individuality, and when one thing is cognised as having a character different from that of another that there is a distinct cognition of individuality. Thus, at the indeterminate stage, there is only the mere awareness of the nature of the thing, because it is not dependent on anything else. It is for this reason that such awareness is not cognisant of a qualificatory relationship among generality, individuality and specific particularity of an object as the cognition of this relationship is preceded by the apprehension of distinction among these three, which is absent in the case of the indeterminate. It is after such apprehension is produced that there appears the determinate which cognises the general and the individual characters of thing, because when a man, at the time of cognising one object recalls another, he has a distinct cognition of the fact that the former is in certain respects similar to, and again, in certain respects dissimilar to, the latter. It is only then that there appears the notion of generality and individuality.[41]

Discussion in this regard is very brief in the *Vyomavatī*. The author gives only one argument of admitting indeterminate knowledge, which is also the main argument given by Śrīdhara. If there is no awareness of the object as qualified by its properties, the knower would not be able to recollect the convention (*saṃketa*) determining the meaning of a word. In other words, the knower would not then be able to remember the particular word denoting the particular object. If the word is not remembered, there cannot be any determinate knowledge, because the precondition for such knowledge is such recollection. Therefore, to justify determinate knowledge itself one would have to admit the indeterminate. Of course, it may be argued that let it be accepted that such recollection only is the cause of determinate knowledge, the object or the contact with it is not a cause of the determinate. The commentator replies that the situation is the same in the case of both the indeterminate and the determinate. In both the cases it is determined through agreement in presence (*anvya*) and agreement in absence (*vyatireka*) that the object is also responsible.[42]

Udayana and his commentator Vardhamāna explain the argument in different terminology.[43] In fact, this argument is accepted by the later writers as the standard argument for admitting indeterminate knowledge.[44] Roughly it is as follows. The precondition for the appearance of a qualificative cognition (*viśiṣṭa–buddhi*) is the knowledge of the qualifier. Unless there is a prior knowledge of the qualifier there cannot be produced any qualificative cognition. All the cases of determinate knowledge are qualificative cognitions. For example, when one has the determinate knowledge 'cow', the qualifier is cowness and the qulificand is the animal called cow. Therefore, previously one must have an unqualified knowledge of cowness, and then only one can have the knowledge of a cow as qualified by the universal of cowness. The indeterminate knowledge must be unqualified. If it also is supposed to be a qualified knowledge or a qualificative cognition, then, the knowledge of qualifier would be necessary in this case also. That subsequent knowledge, if a qualified one, would again presuppose a prior knowledge of the qualifier. If the process goes on in this way, there will occur the fallacy of infinite regress. It is therefore to be admitted that the initial indeterminate awareness is unqualified.

Indeterminate knowledge is followed by determinate knowledge. Praśastapāda gives five forms of such knowledge depending upon the nature of the qualifier.[45] Thus, assisted by the knowledge of a universal, a universal-particular, a substance, a quality and an action (which may have the status of a qualifier), the contact between the self and the mind produces determinate knowledge. The examples also are given one by one. The first is, the substance is existent. Here the universal of existence (*sattā*) is the qualifier. The second example is, it is earth. Here the qualifier is earth-ness, which is both a universal and a particular. The third example is, it has horns. Here the qualifier is the horn, which is a substance. The fourth example is, the cow is white. Here the qualifier is whiteness which is a quality. The last example is, it is moving. Here the qualifier is movement which comes under the category of *karmaṇ*.

It is to be noted that the contact between the self and the mind has been specially mentioned here. But is it really necessary? It has been already stated that for perception contacts among the four are necessary and this particular contact is already included them. Commentators therefore have to offer justification for mentioning it once again. According to Śrīdhara,[46] the idea is to emphasize that the author is going to describe the nature of a different kind of perception, namely, the determinate, as distinguished from the indeterminate. Other commentators however remark that the purpose is to emphasize the fact that such a contact is the non-inherent (*asamavāyin*) cause for any knowledge.

Praśastapāda also states in details how perceptual knowledge in respect of the different qualities is produced.[47] Thus, the conditions necessary for the perception of the four qualities of colour, taste, smell and touch are: they must in here in substances composed of many parts, they must be characterised by their own special character and the substances in which they inhere must come in contact with the sense-organs. The knowledge of each particular quality again is possible through only a particular sense organ. There is a law of restriction that one particular quality is perceived by one particular sense organ only, and not by any other.

The necessity of the first condition is obvious. If the substance itself is not perceived, the question of perceiving its qualities does not arise. It has been already pointed out that a substance to be perceptible must be composed of many parts.

The third condition also is similar. If the substance having the quality does not come in contact with the sense organ there can be no possibility of perceiving the quality.

According to Śrīdhara,[48] the second condition actually justifies the law of restriction with regard to a sense organ and a quality. For example, it is well known that colour is perceived by the visual sense only. Even if there may be a contact between some other quality and the visual organ, the quality would not be perceived. The ground for this is the presence of the universal *rūpatva* in colour only and not in any other quality. Therefore *rūpatva* also should be considered as a cause for the perception of colour by the visual organ.

As the special character of a quality Śrīdhara takes here the universal present in the quality. But another commentator differs and states that the special character means the properties like manifestedness etc.,[49] the presence or absence of which under different conditions may make a quality perceptible or imperceptible.

Sound (*śabda*) is admitted to be a quality and it has some special characteristics. As regards its perception, Praśastapāda says that it is produced by contacts among the three (namely, self, mind and sense– organ) by the auditory sense itself when it is located there.[50] According to the Nyāya-Vaiśeṣika, sound is exclusively the quality of the substance called *ākāśa*, which is eternal and all-pervasive. The auditory sense organ is actually that particular part of *ākāśa* as is enclosed by the ear-hole. A sense-object contact in this case would mean a relation between a sound and the particular part of *ākāśa*. Again, since sound is a quality and *ākāśa* is its substance or substratum the relation between them would be inherence. When a sound ultimately makes its appearance within the ear-hole it is perceived.[51]

So far Praśastapāda has discussed the perception of qualities which are known by one sense organ only. This is followed by a list of qualities which are known by two sense organs, namely, the visual and the tactual. Such qualities are number, magnitude, separateness, conjunction, disjunction, proximity, non-proximity, viscidity, fluidity and velocity. However, to be perceptible they must inhere in substances which are themselves perceptible. Lastly, for the perception of the internal qualities (e.g. desire, knowledge etc.) all of which belong to the self only a conjunction between the two, namely, the self and the mind is sufficient. All these qualities can be produced only in the self and they can be known only by the internal sense organ or the mind.[52]

Though Praśastapāda clearly recognises the necessity of a contact between the sense organ and the object, he has not specified the nature of the contact which may vary according to the nature of the object of knowledge. For example, the nature of the contacts for the perceptions of a substance and a universal present in a quality which belongs to that substance are not exactly the same. While explaining Gautama's definition of perception, Uddyotakara has specified six types of sense-object contact which account for the perception of all the Vaiśeṣika categories. All the commentators of Praśastapāda have taken it for granted that these six contacts are also admitted by the Vaiśeṣikas and they have explained the perception of substance etc. on the basis of them.[53]

Śrīdhara however refers to a view held by others, which is slightly different. According to it, the two direct forms of relation, namely, conjunction and inherence, should be considered as the contacts and there is no necessity of admitting some further indirect forms of relation as contacts. Thus, a substance is perceived by a contact in the form of conjunction and the qualities or the universal present in that substance also should be perceived by the same contact. Some objects are by nature such that they may be perceived even due to a contact not with themselves but with something else. Of course, an objection may raised. If a quality is admitted to be perceptible even if there is no actual contact with it, then the quality of sound also may be said to be perceived by any sense organ. In answer, it is pointed out that a contact with the substratum of the particular quality is necessary. In the case of sound the substratum *ākāśa* is not in contact with any sense organ.[54]

The perception of the third category, *karmaṇ*, is stated to be exactly similar to that of the qualities like number etc.[55] That is, an action can be perceived by the two sense organs, the visual and the tactual, if they inherc in substances which are perceptible.

From the comments of Śrīdhara and Udayana it appears that there is dispute about the perceptibility of action. As Śrīdhara notes,[56] some argue that it is not possible to speak of the perception of action, because when a substance moves what one experiences is nothing but conjunctions and disjunctions and no separate category is apprehended which may be admitted as *karmaṇ*. In such a case, an awareness in the form it is moving is due to the action which is not perceptible but inferred from the gradual conjunctions and disjunctions.

Refuting the contention Śrīdhara says that if an action be imperceptible and only to be inferred from conjunction and disjunction, then, since conjunctions and disjunctions always belong to two substances (e.g. a moving object and the ground it moves upon), the action of moving should be inferred and admitted to be present in the other substance (ground) also. As a matter of fact, however, we find that when a monkey moves from the top of the tree to its root, and again from the root to the top, we have no such notion as that the tree moves, though the tree also is equally the locus of the conjunctions and disjunctions.

The opponent may point out that action is not inferred with reference to the tree because a monkey has certain other conjunctions also, as for instance, those with the points of space and the like, and these other conjunctions are not known to be brought about by any action of the tree.

Śrīdhara replies that if such be the case, then, for the sake of these other conjunctions it may be necessary to assume some other action of the monkey, but in any case it would not be possible to deny the inference of action even in the tree. There is a general rule to the effect that the substratum of the cause and the substratum of the effect should be the same. If this rule is not accepted in one instance, how could one believe in it in other instances and rule out the possibility of deviation?

The opponent may persist and argue that when one has assumed the action of the monkey on the strength of inference from conjunctions and disjunctions, it is found sufficient to explain all such conjunctions of the monkey as those with the tree and those with the points of space. As such, there is no ground for assuming actions on the part of both the monkey and the tree.

Replying to this, Śrīdhara says that when one has to explain something one cannot go by one's imagination, one has to take into consideration the actual order of things. All that is needed for an inference is that whenever the pervaded or the mark is perceived it points to the presence of its pervader or the thing it is concomitant with. Inference is not something like an intelligent human being so that it should operate with reference to some special purpose in view.

Further, if it is assumed that the conjunction and the disjunction of any point in space are the cause for the inference of an action it would be illogical, because they are imperceptible due to the fact that space is beyond the reach of the senses. If, then, action be sought to be inferred from the series of conjunctions and disjunctions of some particular part of the earth-globe, the action of a flying bird would be inexplicable and incomprehensible. It may be argued that the inferential mark in this case is represented by the conjunctions and disjunctions of the light overspreading the atmosphere. But, in that case, there could be no basis or explanation for such notions as 'my arm is throbbing', 'my eyebrow is moving', when they are produced by the sense of touch as controlled by the invisible internal organ, actions which appear in dense darkness because of the action of disordered wind in the body. Moreover, it would not be possible to explain the notion of movement that we have in a very dark and cloudy night with regard to the lightning flash which lasts just for a moment and is not perceived as having any conjunctions or disjunctions.

Udayana also has discussed the problem in some details.[57] His commentator Vardhamāna has noted some of the opponent's arguments for denying the perception of action. The opponent says that what one perceives is only a series of gradual conjunctions and disjunctions and nothing else which may be called action. In fact, even if there were some additional thing in the form of action it would not have been perceived by the senses. The senses have limited power and their function ceases at a particular point. Thus the power of the sense organ would be exhausted by the perception of the series of conjunctions and disjunctions and its function would come to an end, it would not be able to produce further the perception of the action.

This is due to the fact that an action cannot occur without producing conjunctions and disjunctions and one can never be aware of action without being aware of these conjunctions and disjunctions. For example, a person seated in a moving chariot has the awareness 'the chariot is moving', because he has the awareness that he is being placed in different and different parts of space. But the person driving the chariot has no notion of movement, but takes it to be stationery, because he cannot ascertain the different connections with the different parts of space. Therefore, the notion of movement is not perceptual, but only inferential.

Continuing his explanation of the opponent's view, Vardhamāna further notes that even admitting that an action is perceptible, disjunction from the old point of space and conjunction with a new point of space are to be admitted as manifesting it. But in that case the disjunction and the conjunction would not be perceived, because a sense organ has a limited capability and it would lose its capability by perceiving the action, its power would not extend to a further perception of disjunction or conjunction. Moreover, in certain cases it is to be admitted by all that an action cannot be perceived, as in the case of earthquake. As soon as the conjunction with a new point of space is produced the action is destroyed and then, the action cannot be perceived because in spite of the presence of the thing manifesting the thing to be manifested is non-existent.

Besides, the conjunction also can be the cause of manifestation only as being itself known, and not simply by its presence. In that case, there is actually no scope for the perception of the action. The sequence of events would be- first, conjunction with a new point of space is produced; secondly, at the next moment, these will be an awareness of the conjunction and also the absence of the action due to the conjunction, and then, there may be an opportunity for perceiving the action. But such a claim is absurd, because the action itself has been destroyed.

In refutation of the above view, Udayana says that we have first to determine whether a thing is perceptible or imperceptible. If it is proved to be imperceptible beyond doubt then only the question of inferring it on the evidence of some specific events arises. As for example, air is proved to be imperceptible and hence it is inferred on the basis of some specific grounds. But it is not so in the case of action. An action cannot be said to be imperceptible because it is very shortlived, for in that case there would not be any perception of qualities like pleasure, pain etc. Which are all momentary. Nor can it be said to be so because it is destroyed by conjunction with a new point of space, for disjunction also is so destroyed and there will be deviation.

Moreover, it cannot be said that action is inferred from a series of disjunctions from old points of space and conjunction with new points of space, because then there will be no awareness of movement. For example, in the case of the sun there is an awareness of being related with different points of space, yet no one has ever an awareness in the form 'the sun moves'. It may be argued that actually in the case of the sun there is no awareness of being related to different points of space, because space is an imperceptible substance. But it would be improper as in that case one would have to admit that in deep darkness a firefly's contacts with different points of space also are imperceptible and as a result its movement would not be inferred.

Of course, it may be argued that there may be an awareness of conjunctions with and disjunctions from the light of the firefly, and not the insect itself. But, then, the same principle may be applied to the case of the sun also and there should be an awareness of the sun's movement. It may be objected further that the sun's light is very widespread and hence conjunctions with and disjunction from it are not apprehended. Hence, the difficulty does not arise. But Udayana contends that the same may be said to be true of the firefly's light on the ground that it is too little. Finally Udayana remarks that if the opponent is determined to accept the position that an action is totally imperceptible, let him not admit any category called action. It would be enough to admit only conjunctions and disjunctions which are perceptible and let it be admitted that the notion of movement is due to them and nothing else.

Next, Praśastapāda comes to be perception of the fourth category, universal (*sāmānya*).[58] According to the Vaiśeṣika, of the six categories only the first four are perceptible, and the last two, namely, particularity and inherence are imperceptible. The condition for the perceptibility of universality is that it should be located in a perceptible locus, and it is perceived by the same sense organ as perceives the locus. For example, a substance is perceived by two senses, the visual and the tactual. So the universal of *sattā* as present in it is perceived by the same. However, as the commentators point out, the contact varies in each case. In the case of the perception of a substance the contact is conjunction, but in the case of the perception of a universal present in it the contact is inherence in what is conjoined. Again, the quality of smell is perceived only by the olfactory sense. So *sattā* as present in it would also be perceived by the same sense organ. But the contact for the perception of smell is inherence in what is conjoined and the contact for the perception of *sattā* there is inherence in what is inhering in the conjoined. The quality of sound is perceived through a special type of contact, namely, inherence and *sattā* as present in it is perceived through the contact of inherence in the inhering. But both are perceived by auditory sense.

Praśastapāda has also made a distinction between the perception of an ordinary person and the perception of a yogi.[59] According to him, the account as given above represents the perception of ordinary persons like us. But he also mentions, though very briefly, the nature of the yogi's perception. So far as his remark is concerned the spatiality in the case of such perception relates to the objects perceived. Objects which are imperceptible for ordinary persons are not so for the yogis. For example, they can have direct awareness of the nature of the things like their own selves, other's selves *ākāśa*, time, space, atoms and the like as well as the qualities, actions, universals and particularities as present in them. The yogis are divided into two classes, *yukta* or those who are constantly in the state of *samādhi* and *viyukta* or those who can be in the state of *samādhi* whenever they wish.

Commentators have elaborated long on the brief remark of Praśastapāda. Śrīdhara points out that the yogis have no perception of the super-sensuous objects until the covering of impurities have been removed from their minds. Thus, while in the state of deep concentration (*samādhi*), the yogis, through the instrumentality of the mind as assisted by *dharma* born of *yoga*, obtain perfectly true conceptions with regard to all the various objects which are ordinarily imperceptible.[60]

Sometimes we may also internally perceive our own selves. But there is a basic difference between such perceptions of an ordinary person and of the yogi. When we perceive the self we perceive it as the doer (*kartṛ*) or the possessor (*svāmin*). But both these characters are attributed to the self because of its connection with some extraneous factor like the body etc., and they are not natural to the self. That is why such notions are admitted to be false by all the systems of philosophy simply because they reveal what is contrary to the true state of things. But the true nature of the self and its essential properties can be known by the yogis.

Śrīdhara has also tried to show how the yogi acquires the knowledge of the same. When the yogi makes up his mind to know the true character of the self as taught in Vedānta, he withdraws his mind from the external sense organs, and fixing it upon a definite part of the self, he continues single-mindedly to practice meditation upon the self. As a result, there is produced such *dharma* as is conducive to the attainment of true knowledge and next, there clearly appears before his mind the real self free from all impositions of the 'I' or the 'mine'. When however he practices meditation with a view to learn the truth with regard to other selves or with regard to space, time etc., there comes about *dharma* having extraordinary power helping him to acquire the true knowledge with regard to those things. Because of the force of this *dharma*, his internal organ moves out of the body and comes in contact with those other selves etc. Finally, through appropriate contacts, the various objects and there qualities are correctly apprehended. Even in the case of the sciences and the arts we find that although there may not be any proper knowledge of them, knowledge is indeed produced when due attention is paid and the mind is fixed in constant meditation upon those subjects.

Thus, Śrīdhara finally claims, that the yogis are capable of such an extraordinary feat is proved by inferential arguments. The collective force of constant contemplation of the self, *ākāśa* and such things is the cause of the true knowledge about them, because it is a particular kind of practice, like the practice of learning the sciences and the arts; the varying grades of the intellect involve in the practice have a certain limit beyond which it does not go, because they are varying grades, like the varying grades of dimension; the limit in the present case would be the true knowledge of the self etc.

This procedure is applicable to the first type of yogi. As to the second type of yogi, it is said, when such a person, having before him all the best of objects and having none of the effective causes dulled in any way comes to have the contact of the four – self, mind, sense organ and the object-and this contact is assisted by *dharma* as produced by yogic practices, then, because of such contact, he comes to have a direct perception of subtle things like the mind, the atom etc., of things hidden from ordinary view like the neither region of serpents, and of distant things, like the region of Brahma etc.

Though the Nyāya-Vaiśeṣikas and some other systems of Indian philosophy admit the yogi or an omniscient being, there is strong opposition to the concept at least from the Mīmāṃsakas. Kumārila Bhaṭṭa has examined and refuted the idea of a yogi elaborately and with strong arguments.[61] Perhaps that is why Śrīdhara is anxious to show yogic perception is possible. Subsequently he has also examined and refuted some arguments denying the possibility of the yogi. Udayana also has proceeded in a similar manner in the present context.

Perception is a form of pramāṇa and as is well known, the term *pramāṇa* etymologically means an instrument producing a particular effect. Praśastapāda next proceeds to show, in the case of perception, what exactly constitutes the instrument and what the effect.[62] Here also one has to proceed step by step. In other words, what is the instrument in relation to a particular effect may itself become the effect in relation to some other particular instrument. Thus, when one has the cognition of the common universal of *sattā* and the particular universals of *dravyatva*, *guṇatva* etc., the instrument would be a mere knowledge without revealing any qualifier, the object of knowledge would be things like the substance etc., the agent would be the particular self and the effect would be a valid knowledge about the substance etc. But when one acquires this mere knowledge, this instrument would be the sense-object contact as without having any assistance from another knowledge.

It is somewhat difficult to understand what exactly is the significance of the cryptic remarks of Praśastapāda here. The commentators seem to explain the whole thing with the concepts of determinate (*savikalpaka*) and indeterminate (*nirvikalpaka*) perceptions[63]. Indeterminate perception does not reveal any qualifier-qualificand relation. But it is produced as soon as the sense organ comes in contact with the object. It is a kind of 'just an awareness' of an object without any reference to any kind of qualification. In other words, in the case of such knowledge, the contact is the instrument and the awareness is the effect. But this awareness leads to another awareness revealing a qualifier-qualificand relation between a property and its locus. This is determinate perception. In the case of such knowledge the instrument is not only the contact but also the awareness. Thus, in a sense, the indeterminate knowledge, considered an effect earlier, becomes later an instrument. Since both the forms of knowledge are perceptual the contact must be there, but the difference lies in the fact that in the former no assistance is provided by a knowledge, while in the latter it is.

Continuing the discussion Praśastapāda refers to an alternative view. He says:

"Or, perception as *pramāṇa* means that knowledge which is produced in respect of all objects due to the contact of the four and which is non-erroneous and non-verbal. The objects of right knowledge are the categories like substance etc. The knower is the self. The resulting right knowledge is the awareness of the characters of pleasantness (*guṇa*), unpleasantness (*doṣa*) and indifference (*madhyastha*)"[64]

Thus it appears that the final determinate knowledge also may give rise to another particular form of knowledge. Taking this knowledge as an effect, the determinate knowledge may be considered as an instrument. Praśastapāda does not elaborate upon the nature of the knowledge or the effect produced by the determinate knowledge. It is also not easy to understand his terminology and it is difficult to say what he means exactly here by the terms *guṇa*, *doṣa*, and *madhyastha*.

The commentators are however unanimous in accepting that the three forms of knowledge mentioned here are knowledge producing activity for obtainment (*upādāna-buddhi*), knowledge producing activity for avoidance (*hana-buddhi*) and knowledge producing neither of the above forms of knowledge (*upekṣa-buddhi*).[65] These three forms of knowledge are clearly mentioned by the commentator of the NS, Vātsyāyana.[66] It is possible that Praśastapāda also refers to then, but adopts a different terminology. The commentators must have been influenced by the comments of Vātsyāyana and in the absence of any definite hint from the text itself found it easy to follow the line clearly indicated by Vātsyāyana.

Roughly, the position is as follows. According to Nyāya-Vaiśeṣika, objects may be divided into three classes. Some of the objects are desirable (*upādeya*), i.e. objects which one is willing to obtain. Some objects are opposite in nature, undesirable (*heya*), i.e. objects which one is willing to avoid.

Finally, there are objects for which one feels neither attraction nor repulsion, but remains indifferent. When one acquires a determinate knowledge which specifies the nature of the object one is led to a specific form of activity depending upon the nature of the object as mentioned above. This activity is actually due to an awareness produced by the determinate knowledge.

The process in the case of *upādāna-buddhi* may be described. First one acquires through the sense object contact an awareness about a desirable object; next, one has a recollective awareness that earlier pleasure was produced by an object of this kind; next, there is another specific form of knowledge, namely, this object is also of that kind. (This knowledge is called *parāmarśa*.) This knowledge again leads to a further ascertainment that therefore it also would be the cause of pleasure. Finally, there is *upādāna-buddhi*, namely, since this object is determined to be a cause of pleasure it must be a desirable one. Similar processes are to be accepted for the other two forms of knowledge.

From the other texts of the Nyāya-Vaiśeṣikas and those of the other schools of Indian philosophy it appears that there is controversy regarding such forms of knowledge-whether they can be actually accepted as perceptual awareness.[67] For example, it has been objected that there is a long gap between the sense object contact and the appearance *upādāna-buddhi*. Moreover, according to Nyāya-Vaiśeṣika, knowledge is a momentary quality; it is produced, it exists and it is destroyed. So many pieces of knowledge have to appear during the interval. How can the final knowledge be said to be perceptual in nature? The author of the *Vyomavatī* comments very briefly that it is so indirectly. The idea seems to be that though there is a long gap the indispensable role of the sense organ or contact with it cannot be denied and hence it is to be considered as perceptual.[68]

Śrīdhara mentions further that there are some who interpret the awareness of pleasantness etc. in a different manner. According to them, *guṇa-darśana* is not the same as *upādāna-buddhi*. Thus, the awareness of the character of pleasantness is the knowledge determining an object as the cause of pleasure. Similarly, the awareness of the character of unpleasantness means the knowledge determining an object as the cause of suffering, and the awareness of the character of indifference means the knowledge determining an object neither as a cause of pleasure nor as a cause of suffering. As soon as there is an awareness of the true nature of an object one recollects the good effect produced by it, specifies it as the cause of pleasure and there is a knowledge which produces an activity for obtaining it. All this takes place very quickly, independent of any idea of invariable concomitance, immediately after the nature of the object has been ascertained, because of one's skill acquired by constant practice. Hence it must be considered to be the effect of the determinate knowledge. Although many steps are involved in the process, in the case of an experienced person there is no delay between the determinate knowledge and *upādāna-buddhi*. So both should be taken as perceptual knowledge.[69]

As we have already noted, in Nyāya the role of the sense-object contact is considered the most vital in the case of perception. The Vaiśeṣika does not deny the fact, but lays more stress on the joint activity of the sense, self and object. The Nyāya definition of perception is also more elaborate. According to Gautama, the essential characteristics of perception as a form of valid knowledge are: (i) it is produced from sense-object contact; (ii) it is non-verbal (*avyapadeśya*); (iii) it is non-deviating (*avyabhicārin*); and (iv) it is of a definite character (*vyavasāyātmaka*). Commentators have discussed about the utility of each of the terms, though there is some difference of opinion in the matter.[70]

The first characteristic distinguishes perception from all other forms of valid knowledge. In other cases, the sense-object contact is not a necessary factor. According to Vātsyāyana, the second characteristic is included in the definition to refute the view that all cognitions are verbal or due to words, which is identified by some as the grammarian's view. The third characteristic, absence of deviation, is the essential mark of not only perception but of valid knowledge is general. It is mentioned to exclude perceptual error from the category of perception. Lastly, the fourth characteristic is added to exclude doubt from the category of perception.

Vācaspati's interpretation is different. He thinks that the exclusion of doubt is possible by the third characteristic. In fact, the second and the fourth characteristics do not point to any general character of perception but to its divisions, namely, the indeterminate and the determinate. Praśastapāda also mentions the two characteristics of 'non-verbal' and 'non-deviating'. However he does not do so while explaining the general nature of perception. He refers to them when, according to commentators, he is referring to *upādāna-buddhi* etc. The remarks of both Gautama and Praśastapāda are very brief and it is difficult to be certain about their implications.

Praśastapāda clearly mentions that the mind also is a sense organ. But, as it is well known, there is evidence of controversy in the case of Nyāya. Gautama does not include mind in the list of sense organs. Buddhists have taken exception to this and strongly object that in the Nyāya view mind cannot be a sense organ. Of course, Vātsyāyana has tried to refute such a claim. Nyāya admits the internal perception of the qualities like pleasure, pain etc. So it cannot but accept mind as a sense organ.[71]

Vātsyāyana argues that Gautama does not mention mind in the list of external senses because it differs from them in certain important respects. The external senses are made of elements (*bhūta*), are restricted to their own objects and are characterised by the qualities like smell etc., the perceptions of which they yield. Mind, on the contrary, does not share any of these peculiarities and is quite opposite in nature. Finally, Vātsyāyana takes the help of *tantra-yukti*,[72] which means when somebody expresses his own view, but does not refute the view of another that does not contradict his own view he accepts by implication the said view of the other.

We have clear mention of *upādāna-buddhi* etc. in the commentary of Vātsyāyana itself. The Nyāya commentators have discussed much about the possibility of such knowledge. The division of perception into indeterminate and determinate also is much discussed by later commentators, though there is no clear reference to then in the earliest basic texts. Later commentators have to tackle with many other problems related to perception as the Buddhists start to criticise strongly the various positions of the Nyāya. Thus the commentators discuss whether the senses act after coming in actual contact with the object or not, whether pleasure etc. represent different kinds of qualities or are essentially the same as awareness, and so on.

In the case of the Vaiśeṣika, we are not very fortunate because the literature is not very extensive. We have no early commentary or independent works clarifying the Vaiśeṣika views. The commentaries available are much later and they have a tendency to explain the problems in the light of Nyāya conclusions reached after deliberations by the commentators through the ages.

NOTES & REFERENCES

1. Vs, 3.1.18., 3.2.1., 3.2.1., 5.2.15. etc.
2. Vs, 5.2.15.
3. Vs, (C), p.169.
4. Ibid, p.174.
5. On NS 1.1.4.
6. NS, 2.1.21.
7. On ibid.
8. NS 2.1.23. According to Vācaspati, it represents the opponent's view, but others do not think so.
9. NS, 2.1.24 and also 1.1.10.
10. NS, 2.1.26.
11. NS, 2.1.27.
12. NS, 2.1.28.
13. On NS, 2.1.29-30.
14. VS, 4.1.6.
15. *Upaṣkāra* on ibid.
16. VS, 4.1.8. and *Upaṣkāra* there on.
17. NS, 3.1.38 and commentary there on.
18. VS, 4.1.9. and *Upaṣkāra* thereon.
19. VS, 4.1.11.
20. VS, 9.1.11-13 and *Upaṣkāra*.
21. There is controversy regarding the nature of the compound in the term. See *Vyomavatī* (p.137), *Kiraṇāvalī* (p.530) and NK (p.444).
22. *Vyomavatī*, p.138. Obviously, the reference is to NS 1.1.4. Thus, the commentator follows Vātsyāyana.
23. *Vyomavatī*, pp. 138-139. From the commentaries on NS, it appears that there is a lot of controversy regarding the actual significance of the expression. See, for example, NM and NVTT.
24. Ibid, p. 139. These contacts are first enumerated in NV on NS 1.1.4.

25. NK, p. 443.

26. Ibid.

27. For a discussion of the controversy, see, for example, NM, pp. 70-71.

28. NK, pp. 443-444.

29. NK, p. 445.

30. NK, pp 445-446.

31. *Kiraṇāvalī*, p.530.

32. Ibid. It is also found in later works like TCM, TB and PP.

33. PPbh, p.443.

34. *Kiraṇāvalī*, p.531.

35. See *Siddhāntamuktavalī* on the discussion of the fifth *anyathāsiddha*.

36. PPbh, p. 443.

37. NK, pp. 444-445.

38. Ibid.

39. The Buddhists think that indeterminate perception alone is valid, but the grammarians think that determinate perception alone is possible. The controversy is quite old for it appears that we have evidences of it in the commentary of Vātsyāyana. All the later Nyāya-Vaiśeṣika commentators discuss the controversy at length. For example see NK, pp.449-459.

40. NK, p. 446.

41. Ibid, pp. 446-448.

42. *Vyomavatī*, p.141.

43. *Kiraṇāvalī*, p.532.

44. For example, TCM, p.817.

45. PPbh, P. 447.

46. NK, p.448.

47. PPbh, p.459 f.

48. NK, p.459f.

49. *Vyomavatī*, p.142 see also *Kiraṇāvalī*, p.535.

50. PPbh p.460.

51. Cf. *vici-taraṅga-nyāya* or *kadamba-mukula-nyāya*.

52. PPbh, pp. 460ff.

53. For example, NK, p.463.

54. NK, p.464.

55. PPbh, p.464.

56. NK, pp.460-462.

57. *Kiraṇāvalī*, pp.536 ff.

58. PPbh, p.464.

59. PPbh, .p.464 ff.

60. NK, pp.465 ff.

61. For a good account of the controversy, see PKM, pp247 ff. and NM, pt. (i), pp.95 ff.

62. PPbh, pp. 471 ff.

63. For example, NK, pp. 471 ff.

64. PPbh pp. 474 ff.

65. For example, NK, p. 475 f.

66. On NS, 1.1.3.

67. NM, pt. (i) pp.62f.

68. *Vyomavatī*, p.147.

69. NK, p.476.

70. NS 1.1.4 and the commentaries thereon.

71. At the end of his commentary on NS, 1.1.4 Vātsyāyana has given arguments for not mentioning *manas* in the list of senseorgans.

72. Cf. the last section of the Arthaśāstra which discusses *tantra-yukti* in details. For example, NVTT, NM etc.

Chapter Three

Inference

All the systems of Indian Philosophy, except the Cārvaka, accept inference (*anumāna*) as a source of valid knowledge. This has also made it necessary to discuss the nature of inference itself as a special topic. Thus, even in their early works, the different systems offer their own accounts of inference and problems connected with it.

The Vaiśeṣika is also no exception. From, the very beginning, almost on every step, the VS points to many conclusions which are reached through inference. Thus the importance of inference in the Vaiśeṣika system can hardly by denied.

Moreover, most probably we meet with the earliest classification of the systems of Indian philosophy in the *Arthaśāstra* of Kauṭilya. According to him, the branch of knowledge known as *ānvīkṣikī* consists of three systems, namely, Sāṃkhya, Yoga and Lokāyata.[1] Basically, this branch of learning represents the one which proceeds on the basis of inference.[2] The Yoga system, it has been argued by many scholars, is here the same as the Vaiśeṣika.[3] If we accept this interpretation, inference becomes an essential part of Vaiśeṣika epistemology and it should be almost obligatory for the system to offer its own account of the nature and process of inference.

Inference in The VS

While trying to have some idea about Kaṇada's view on inference and allied problems, we should remember two points. First, the VS is not a very systematic work. It gives its own ideas about inference, but it may be rather scanty. Comments are made and illustrations are given not always with the express purpose of discussing inference itself, but in passing, the main topic of discussion being something different. In fact, the relevant points are found scattered over the different chapters and sections of the whole work.

Secondly, to have an idea of Kaṇāda's notion of inference we have to take into consideration both theory and practice. We may have information by following the implications of the *sūtras* which treat of inference in a general way and also by examining the inferential process he makes use of to arrive at a certain conclusion.

For inference the term used by Kaṇāda is *laiṅgika*, literally relating to or proceeding from a linga or mark. It occurs in the tenth chapter,[4] in a *sutra* which states that doubt (*saṃśaya)* and ascertainment (*nirṇaya)* are produced by perception and inference, which are also the only forms of *pramāṇa* admitted by the Vaiśeṣika. The context, according to commentators, is showing the distinction of pleasure (*sukha*) and pain (*duḥkha)* from knowledge (*jñāna).* The term generally used to indicate an inferential mark is *linga*, though the word *hetu* also occurs in a few cases.[5] There is also one *sūtra* declaring that the terms *hetu, apadeśa, liṅga, pramāṇa* and *karaṇa* are synonymous.[6] The context here is indicating the wellknown Vaiśeṣika conclusion that verbal testimony, a separate *pramāṇa* according to Nyāya and others, is actually a form of inference.

In the NS Gautama gives a clear definition of inference, but in the VS Kanada does not do so. But there are remarks in his work which have been explained as pointing to such a definition. For example, after enumerating some cases in which the inference of one from the other is possible, Kaṇāda, giving the ground for legitimacy, says that a valid mark or its statement is dependent upon *prasiddhi*.[7]

If by *prasiddhi* we take some fact universally known, some kind of a general rule concerning two things established on the basis of repeated observation, we may arrive at the ground of inference later wellknown as *vyāpti, pervasion*. If however we equate *prasiddhi* with previous perception (*pūrva-pratīti)* we may have a definition of inference very similar to the one offered by Gautam.[8]

In the context of inference two *sūtras* of Kaṇāda, one in the third chapter and the other in the ninth, particularly the latter, have been treated with greater importance, and accordingly, are often referred to and discussed.[9] Both of them enumerate cases of possible inference and each gives four cases. But three are common to both and thus, we have actually a total of five cases. They are: (i) the cause-effect *(kārya-kāraṇa)*, (ii) the conjunct (*saṃyogin*), (iii) the inherent (*samavāyin*), (iv) the co-inherent in the same substance *(ekārtha-samavāyin)* and (v) the opposite (*virodhin*). Kaṇāda himself does not give illustrations, but they are provided by the commentators.

The examples of the first are wellknown. When we infer fire from smoke we infer the cause from the effect. Again, when there is an inference of sound on the part of the deaf from the striking of a drum with a stick, we infer the effect from the cause. An example of the second is: the body has skin, because it is corporeal. Skin is a natural element of the body capable of growth and decay, and is neither a cause nor an effect of the body, but only produced together with the body and invariably conjoined with it. An example of the third would be; *ākāśa* has magnitude (*parimāṇa*), because it has substance-ness *dravyatva*, just like a jar. Here the inferable property is magnitude and it is sought to be proved by substance-ness, a property inhering in *ākāśa.* An example of the fourth would be the inference of a particular colour as located in a particular substance from a particular taste as located in the same substance.[10]

The fifth has been elaborated by Kaṇāda himself in a few *sūtras*. When there is opposition (*virodha*) between two we may infer presence (*bhūta*) from absence (*abhūta*), e.g. presence of cloud-wind conjunction from absence of rain; or absence from presence, e.g. absence of rain from presence of cloud-wind conjunction; or, presence from presence, e.g. the presence of a mongoose hidden behind a bush from the presence of an agitated snake.[11]

As regards the classification of inference or inferential mark, we hardly get anything definite in the VS. Depending upon its account of the inferences of air and self, we may speak of two kinds of inferential mark, *dṛṣṭa* or the seen and *adṛṣṭa* or the unseen. When the mark and the inferable property are both perceptible and it is possible to ascertain the concomitance by direct observation, the mark would be the seen, e.g. peculiar horns, the hump, a peculiar tail or the dewlap for the inference of a cow. When it is not so and even if the mark is perceptible, but the inferable thing is not, the mark would be the unseen, e.g. touch for the inference of air.[12]

In the NS we have a clear reference to three forms of inference, namely *pūrvavat*, *śeṣavat* and *sāmānyato-dṛṣṭa*, but there is no hint as to their nature and application.[13] Vātsyāyana offers alternative explanations for each variety. According to the first interpretation, the first type stands for an inference of the effect from the cause and the second type stands for an inference of the cause from the effect. Thus it is easy to see that, though the terminology is different, these two types are identical with the ones mentioned by Kaṇāda as based upon the cause-effect relation.

According to Vātsyāyana's second interpretation, *pūrvavat* is as follows. Two objects are first perceived as invariably related with each other. Later on, an object similar to one them is perceived elsewhere and it leads to the inference there of the object similar to the other. Smoke and fire are perceived in the kitchen etc. as invariably related. Afterwards similar smoke is perceived in the hill and similar fire is inferred there. This is perhaps the commonest form of inference and it may be easily considered equivalent to Kaṇada's inference with a *dṛṣṭa* mark.

The two terms *pūrvavat* and *śeṣavat* are not actually used by Kaṇāda. But the case with *sāmānyato dṛṣṭa* is different, because it occurs twice in the VS, in two *sūtras* of exactly the same form.[14] The context is the inference of air and the inference of self. From the examples two points about these kinds of inference are clear. First, it is exclusively employed to prove an imperceptible thing. When there is no perceptible mark for the inference of a thing, we have to take the help of such an inference. Secondly, it proves a thing only generally and not specifically. By itself, it is not capable of final specification, but has to depend on the subsequent assistance of an accessory for the purpose. Thus in the case of air, assistance is provided by *āgama* and in the case of *ākāśa* as a locus of sound by *pariśeṣa*.[15] It appears that these characteristics are preserved by *sāmānyatodṛṣṭa* later also.

According to Vātsyāyana's second interpretation of *śeṣavat*. It is synonymous with *pariśeṣa*. Kaṇāda mentions *pariśeṣa* at least once, in the inference of *ākāśa* as a distinct substance, as a locus of the quality of sound. He proceeds by way of elimination. First it is shown that sound cannot belong to any of the four substances having touch, namely, earth, water, fire and air. Next it is shown that sound cannot belong either to the self or to the mind, and on the same ground it is established that it cannot belong also to the two other substances, time and space. Sound thus belongs to a new substance, namely, *ākāśa*. According to commentators, here also the first step is a *sāmānyato dṛṣṭa*. establishing generally that sound being a quality must have a substance as its substratum, and in the second step, this substance is proved specifically to be *ākāśa*.[16]

It is interesting to note that Vātsyāyana offers a general definition of *pariśeṣa* which clearly takes note of this procedure based on elimination and moreover, the illustration he gives and explains is typically a Vaiśeṣika view, namely sound belongs to the category of quality.[17] In the NS itself also, we have at least one reference to *pariśeṣa* and that also in the same sense.[18] In his commentary thereon, Vātsyāyana quotes the definition of *pariśeṣa* given earlier and shows how knowledge is proved to be a quality of the self alone, as the possibility of its belonging to any other substance is gradually rejected.

Though there are difficulties in forming definite conclusions on the basis of the VS and its much later commentaries it may be rightly concluded that so far as inference is concerned some of the basic ideas originated with the VS and they were adopted and elaborated by later authorities.

Definition of Inference According to Praśastapāda

Like the author of the VS Praśastapāda also uses the term *laiṅgika* to indicate inference or inferential knowledge. His definition is a simple one, based on the literal meaning of the term, namely that which is produced (*sañjāyamāna*) by the knowledge (*darśana*) of a mark (*liṅga*).[19] Naturally, later commentators have elaborated the definition in their own ways.

According to some, this definition may appear to be too wide, because the knowledge of a mark may produce also an impression (*saṃskāra*), an illusion and a doubt. To exclude such forms of cognitions we have to read the definition as occurring under the general section of valid knowledge. In other words, all the essential characteristics of valid knowledge have to be present in the case of knowledge derived from the knowledge of a mark and then only it should be considered as a case of genuine inference.

The difficulty may be avoided in another way also. The adjectives mentioned in the definition of perception, such as, valid, of a definite character and not due to words, may be continued and added here. They will naturally prevent the definition from applying to undesirable cases. Of course, it may be objected that even then the definition is not free from defect. On perceiving a mark one has the recollection of pervasion, i.e. the invariable relation between the mark and the inferable property. Though it is not actually an inference, the definition would apply to it, because it is a form of valid knowledge and is also produced by the perception of a mark. However, the difficulty may be avoided, again, by borrowing some terms used in the case of the definition of perception. It has been stated earlier that perceptual knowledge is produced in respect of objects like the substance etc. which are actually present there. In the case of recollection, the object is not present there. Thus, the definition will not be applicable to such knowledge.[20]

Thus, finally, inference is knowledge which is not illusory and the instrument of it is the totality of the causes including the knowledge called *parāmarśa*. Alternatively, following the definition that the instrument is the most efficient one of the causes, the knowledge called *parāmarśa* itself may be considered to be the instrument.

According to Śrīdhara, every term in the brief definition of inference is significant.[21] The actual word used by Praśastapāda to indicate the knowledge of the mark is *darśana*, which stands for perceptual knowledge. But inference cannot simply be defined as knowledge produced by the *perception* of a mark because the knowledge of the mark may be derived through some other *pramāṇa* and then also we can have valid inferential knowledge. For example, one sitting inside a room may here the roar of the cloud in the sky and infers that it is going to rain. Here the knowledge of the mark, namely, the cloud, is not perceived, but inferred on hearing the sound. Similarly, the knowledge of the mark may be derived through verbal testimony also. Somebody coming from outside may inform someone sitting inside that clouds have gathered in the sky. From this knowledge the person sitting inside may infer the possibility of rain. Śrīdhara therefore points out that the word *darśana* is to be taken in a wider sense to include all forms of valid knowledge.

Of course, an impression also is produced from the knowledge of a mark, though it cannot be included in the category of inference. The difficulty is easily avoided by stating that since the definition occurs under the general section of knowledge it would only apply to some form of knowledge and not to any other quality.

The difficulty of the definition being applicable to doubt and error is solved by Śrīdhara in a different way. In the definition, Praśastapāda uses the term *sañjāyamāna*, and not simply *jāyamāna*. The prefix *sam* meaning 'true', or 'real' serves to exclude doubt, error and recollective cognition. Thus the implication is that inference is that form of knowledge which truly really or rightly proceeds from the cognition of the mark. Any form of knowledge which has the characteristic of being produced rightly is produced also as revealing the true nature of an object, because it is the very nature of all valid cognitions. Doubt and error also reveal an object, but not as the object is in reality. Hence, the definition cannot apply to them. Recollective cognition also does not really reveal an object, because it is dependent upon a previous presentative cognition *(anubhava)*.

Incidentally, Śrīdhara criticises the view of the author of *Vyomavatī*, who seems to exclude recollective cognition on the ground that it is not produced by an object. Śrīdhara argues that this is not proper, because in that case some valid forms of inference, namely, the inferences of the past and the future objects would be unduly excluded. As in the case of recollective cognition, the objects themselves are not present in such cases also.[22]

Śrīdhara also takes exception to the *Vyomavatī's* explanation that doubt and error are excluded by the fact of the definition appearing under the section of *vidyā*, while these two are forms of *avidyā*, on the ground that so long as we can get at the desired implication from the sentence (*vākya*) itself, we need not have recourse to implications derived from the context (*prakaraṇa*). The idea is as follows. The undue application of the definition to doubt and error is to be prevented. According to Śrīdhara, it is done by the prefix *sam*, while, according to the *Vyomavatī*, it is to be done by reading the definition in the context of valid knowledge. In the former case, the implication is derived from *vākya* and in the latter from *prakaraṇa*. But the accepted rule is that *vakya* is stronger than *prakaraṇa*.[23]

Udayana notes that Praśastapāda gives the definition of not the instrument (*karaṇa*), but of the result (*phala*).[24] He further points out that the term *anumana* may be derived in two ways, as signifying *bhāva* and as signifying *karaṇa*. Thus, the term means either inferential knowledge (*anumiti*) or the instrument of such knowledge (*anumāna*). Rightly speaking, the definition of the instrument should have been given, because the term *pramāṇa* is definitely derived in the sense of the instrument. However, the instrument is actually a form of *kāraka*, which is essentially connected with an action. Thus, even if the instrument of inference is not stated, there is no harm, because it has been stated how the act of inferring takes place, and it is sufficient to explain the nature of the instrument.

So far as the exclusion of impression, error and doubt is concerned, Udayana is in agreement with Śrīdhara. He also takes the term *darśana* in a wider sense and says that the knowledge of the mark leading to inference may be either perceptual or inferential or even recollective. According to the Vaiśeṣika, verbal testimony is only a form of *anumāna* and not a separate *pramāṇa*. Knowledge derived through verbal testimony is to be included in *anumitānumāna*. He also comments that although the term *sañjāyamāna* points to the present time, it is not implied that the object has to be present at the time of inference; it may as well be past or future. The real implication is that the knowledge should reveal the object as it really it.

Characteristics of A Valid Mark

After defining inference as knowledge derived through the cognition of a mark, Praśastapāda, following a natural and logical order, goes on to mention the essential characteristics of a valid mark. However, he says that this is the view offered by Kāśyapa.[25]

Thus, to be valid, first, a mark should be present in the

thing to be inferred (*anumeya*), secondly, it should be present in things where the inferable property is present and thirdly, it should not be present in things where the inferable property is absent. A mark with these characteristics is capable of producing inferential knowledge.

Almost all the systems of Indian philosophy accept inference as a source of valid knowledge. But naturally they are not unanimous in respect of the various aspects of inference. Thus, there is some controversy about what really constitutes the object of inference.[26] The term *anumeya* or *sādhya* may be used in different senses. It may mean either a property (or an object treated as the property of a thing) or the thing itself as qualified by that property. For example, from the mark, smoke, one may infer either fire (as a property of a hill) or the hill itself as having the fire. In the second sense, the term actually stands for *pakṣa*. While stating the first characteristic, Praśastapāda takes the word in this sense.

But while stating the second and the third characteristics, Praśastapāda takes the word in the first sense. The mark should be present in the instances where the inferable property also is definitely known to be present. In other words, the mark should be present in *sapakṣa*. Thirdly, the mark should not be present in any instance where the inferable property is absent. In other words, the third characteristics means that the mark should be absent from *vipakṣa*.

It is clear that here Praśastapāda is following rather the Buddhist tradition.[27] In the Nyāya tradition we come across two additional characteristics of a valid mark, namely, absence of contradiction (*abādhitatva*) and not having a counteracting mark (*asatpratipakṣatva*). Commentators have tried to justify the absence of these two in Praśastapāda's enumeration and have tried to show that there is no contradiction with the Nyāya view.

The author of *Vyomavatī* raises the point.[28] He says that instances of inference may be cited where the mark satisfies all the three conditions mentioned above, but still they are not cases of valid inference. One of the illustrations given by him is: Fire in the form of a 'whole' (*avayavin*) is not hot, because it is non-eternal, like a pot. A whole is always non-eternal. Substances, namely, earth and water, when they are in the form of wholes are not hot and non-eternal. The *vipakṣa* here is represented by only the fire-atoms. But non-eternality is not present in them. Therefore, according to the tradition of Praśastapāda, it should be a valid case of inference. But the fact is that it is not so, because actually the absence of hotness is proved in fire by the tactual sense. In other words, there is contradiction by perception.

Secondly, one may put forward the inference that sound is eternal, because the property of a non-eternal thing is not ascertained in it, like *ākāśa*. Here also the three essential characteristics are available, but no valid inference is possible, because there is the possibility of a counter-inference, namely, sound is non-eternal, because the property of an eternal thing is not ascertain in it, like the pot. The two inferences oppose each other. Both have all the three characteristics. But, with reference to the same sound, the first tries to establish eternality and the second non-eternality. Hence none can establish its inferable property.

The commentator's explanation is rather very simple. It is clear that in his view these two additional characteristics are to be accepted and mentioned. Though they are not expressly stated, they can be easily gathered by the term *ca* used in the verse, the purpose of which is to collect or add further information.

The commentator also notes an answer as given by others. Praśastapāda has admitted a different set of faults in the case of inferential formulation, namely, faults related to the statement of thesis (*pratijñā-doṣa*). The inference mentioned above is an instance of being contradicted by perception and suffers from such a fault. No such inference can be put forward because here the statement of thesis is contradicted by perception. In fact, there the same illustration has been given by Praśastapāda himself. It is not therefore necessary to admit the additional characteristic of absence of contradiction to invalidate such cases, because they are already rejected by the said fault.

This view is not accepted by the commentator. He says that the speciality in the case of a contradicted mark consists in the fact that a mark is put forward after an unfit *pakṣa* has been stated earlier. That is why it is also known as a mark which is stated after the proper time has elapsed (*kālātyayapadiṣṭa*). Therefore, it is immaterial whether the statement of thesis is faulty or not.

The opponent may argue that there is an opposition between contradiction (*bādha*) and concomitance (*avinābhāva*). The question is, in an inference said to be suffering from contradiction, is concomitance actually present or not? If the mark is really concomitant with the inferable property, then, it can never be present without the other and as such, the possibility of contradiction would not be there. On the other hand, if it is admitted that really the concomitance is not there, then, it would have to be admitted that the mark may be present without the other, i.e. in a *vipakṣa*. But it means that one of the characteristics is not present in such a case. So the inference becomes wrong. It is therefore not necessary to admit absence of contradiction as an additional characteristic. In answer, it is pointed out that in such a case the concomitance is proved *generally* and it becomes established that all the three characteristics are present But when the *pakṣa* points to an opposite fact the concomitants is disproved only specifically with reference to that particular locus. Hence, the additional characteristic is necessary.

It has also been argued by some that the other characteristic, namely, the absence of a counteracting mark, need not be accepted. Actually, such cases suffer from the fallacy of the unproved (*asiddha*). As we shall see later, there is one variety of this fallacy where the mark put forward is acceptable not to both the parties, but only to either. In the example cited, one is convinced that sound is non-eternal and hence the mark that sound does not show any property belonging to a non-eternal thing is unproved for one. Again, the other is convinced that sound is eternal and hence the mark that sound does not share a property which belongs to eternal things is unproved for him. In short, there is no need to admit a further characteristic.

In answer, the commentator says that in such a case the two opponents are convinced of some general characteristics of sound, but they are not certain about its specific characteristics. So far as the specific characteristics are concerned they are not certain and suffer from a doubt. Both of them being under doubt cannot specifically be sure that the mark offered by the other is unproved. In fact, if any one of them puts forward his thesis on the basis of a *pramāṇa*, the question of being unproved would not arise at all. Thus it is necessary to state a fifth characteristic.

Another commentator, Śrīdhara, has also discussed the problem in his own way.[29] He also first refers to the position of the opponent. According to them, a mark lacking in the two additional characteristics is actually included in the fallacy called the irregular (*anaikāntika*). A counteracted mark is present in such an object with the property to be proved as is liable to being doubted to be a *vipakṣa*. Again, a contradicted mark is present in that which is definitely recognised as a *vipakṣa*.

According to the opponent, the function of the counteracted and the irregular is similar. The former is defined as a mark which, when employed for final ascertainment, gives rise to the suggestion of doubtful alternative possibilities (*prakaraṇa*). In such a case, the absence of the perception of some unique characteristic in either of the alternatives leads to thesis and counter thesis. In the example given above, the characteristic of anything eternal is not perceived in sound and so also is not perceived the characteristic of anything non-eternal. If the characteristic of something eternal is specifically perceived in sound, there can no longer be both thesis and counter thesis and the same is true if there is a perception of the characteristic of something non-eternal. Thus, so long as the one supersedes and suppresses the other it cannot lead to the desired conclusion. Each will act as an obstacle to the other. In short, the mark cannot get to any one (*eka*) definite end (*anta*), which is the essential characteristic of the irregular.

Similarly, a contradicted reason also may be considered as a case of the irregular. The irregular is defined as a mark which is present both in *sapakṣa* and *vipakṣa*. In the case of a contradicted mark, the subject or *pakṣa* is really a *vipakṣa* and the mark is definitely known to be present there.

However, these arguments do not find favour with Śrīdhara. He says that if the inferential potency of the mark consists in the fact of its existing in *sapakṣa* and not existing in *vipakṣa*, while it pervades over the whole of *pakṣa*, then there might be the possibility of an opposition or contradiction in the object possessing the property to be proved. But even then, a counteracted acted mark, by its very power cannot fail to prove what it is meant to prove. If it is unable to prove it, because of an apprehension of contradiction, then, the mark cannot be accepted as capable solely by reason of having the three characteristics. In other words, it would be necessary to lay down another condition for the mark, namely, having no counteracting mark. As long as there is opposition the mark is not a real mark and when there is no opposition then only it becomes a mark.

Continuing his criticism, Śrīdhara argues that the same is true with regard to a contradicted mark also. If the three characteristics were the only conditions of a real mark, then, actually, the mark in the formulation 'fire is not hot, because it is caused' cannot be considered to be irregular since it satisfied all the three conditions. If it be objected that even though fire is caused, it cannot be accepted to be not hot because it is directly known to be hot, then, it would have to be accepted further that the mark in question would prove its conclusion when there is no contradiction by perception and never in the presence of such contradiction. In other words, it would be necessary to lay down another condition for a real mark, namely, that it should have as its objects what is not set aside or negative by a source of valid knowledge.

Finally, therefore, Śrīdhara gives his own solution in a different way. According to him, the term *pakṣa* is synonymous with the term *sādhya*. The term *sādhya* literally means something in respect of which it is proper or fit to offer a mark. When there is the possibility of a counteracting mark proving the opposite of what is sought to be proved, we do not have a real *pakṣa* or *sādhya*, because a thing cannot share two opposite characteristics. In the case of a contradicted mark also we do not have a real *pakṣa* or *sādhya*, because a thing which is already definitely proved to be of a certain nature cannot have a mark applicable to it as proving it to have a different character. In short, Śrīdhara's contention is that in the case of these two kinds of marks we do not have a real *pakṣa* and hence, the first characteristic that a mark must be present in the *pakṣa* is lacking. Therefore, they are excluded because of not having the first of the three characteristics.

Another question with which all the commentators of Praśastapāda have concerned themselves is the special classification of inferences, first formulated by Uddyotakara.[30] According to him, inferences are of three types, namely, only-positive (*anvayin*), only-negative (*vyatirekin*) and positive-negative (*anvaya-vyatirekin*). In later Nyāya works this classification is almost exclusively accepted in preference to the original classification as found in the NS. All the commentators have given illustrations of these kinds of inferences, explained their nature, and tried to show how they can be accommodated in the Vaiśeṣika system.[31]

An example of the only-positive is: the category of *viśeṣa* is nameable, because it is knowable, just like the category of *sāmānya*. Here all things other than the *pakṣa* represent only the *sapakṣa*. Whoever may be the cogniser and whatever the means of cognition there is nothing that is either unknowable or unnamable. That which is unnamable and unknowable by anybody is an absolute non-entity, like a flower blooming in the sky. Such a thing can neither be a *sapaksa* nor a *vipakṣa* because it would have no essential character of its own. However, anything that exists must come under the *sapakṣa*. Thus, in this case, the mark will be lacking in the third characteristic, namely, absence from any *vipakṣa*.

It cannot be argued that the mark here is not a valid one and cannot lead to the right conclusion, because so far as agreement in presence is concerned there is no deviation.

When the presence of one is invariably accompanied by the presence of another and provided that no contrary instance is possible, one can indeed be rightly inferred from the other. That knowability and nameability always co-exists is beyond doubt. It is moreover impossible to suppose that something may be knowable but not nameable. In other words, there is not the slightest possibility of a deviation. Moreover, it is only when there is a *vipakṣa* that the absence from *vipakṣa* can be regarded as one of the conditions for a valid mark, and not when there is absolutely no *vipakṣa*. Hence, knowability is certainly indicative of nameability. It is a case of genuine inference.

Secondly, as an instance of the only-negative, we may mention: The living body is endowed with the self, because it has life (*pramā*). In this case, everything besides the *pakṣa* is *vipakṣa* and there is actually no *sapakṣa*. Even then, the mark is genuine, because it is proved to have never any connection with the absence of the inferable property. In all such substances as the jar etc., it is found that the absence of the self is concomitant with the absence of life, and the cognition of the non-presence of the absence of life leads to the inference of the non-presence of the absence of self.

Of course, it may be objected that if a thing is not known at all, how is it possible to negate it or have a cognition of its absence? A thing may be negated or its absence may be known only on condition that earlier it had been known or had been the object of an affirmation. But the self is something which has nowhere been known. How can one be aware of its absence in the jar or other things?

Obviously Śrīdhara here takes the opponent to be the Buddhists. So he answers the objection with reference to a particular doctrine upheld by the Buddhists. He says that since the opponent holds that all things are devoid of the self (*nairātmya*) he is certainly aware of its absence in the jar also. As to the Vaiśeṣikas, they find that the cause-effect relation between the qualities of *buddhi* etc. and the self is established only in the case of a living body. When it is found further that the effect, e.g. *buddhi*, is absent in the jar, it is naturally concluded that there is in it the absence of the self also which is capable of producing such effects. As for example, in certain circumstances, the absence of smoke leads to the inference of the absence of fire capable of producing smoke.

The opponent may still argue that if such be the case really, the only-negative inference would have no relevance. A relation cannot be ascertained without knowing both the objects related or the relata (*sambandhin*). Thus, in the case of living body, the self is already to be accepted as known as the cause, i.e. as one of the relata. In short, the inference becomes unnecessary. When an action has been duly accomplished by a certain means, any other means for the same appearing subsequently ceases to be of any relevance. In answer, it is pointed out that the presence of the self may be known to the proponent but not to the opponent. The inference becomes necessary to convince the opponent.

In fact, there is no such rule that only the absence of deviation with regard to agreement in presence is conclusive, but the absence of deviation with reference to agreement in absence is not so. Therefore, it is to be accepted that even an only-negative mark is a genuine one.

Thus, it is clear that the above three forms of inference also are genuine. But it is also clear that they are not mentioned in the text, which only states that all the three characteristics of a mark are to be present in a valid one. But, as we see, the only- positive and the only-negative are each lacking in at least one respect. Perhaps the simple answer would have been that actually the Vaiśeṣikas do not admit such a classification. In fact, there are so many systems in Indian philosophy which have criticised this classification strongly. Secondly, in the Nyāya tradition, this classification is first introduced by Uddyotakara. It was accepted and explained by all the later authors and commentators. It may not be possible historically also for Praśastapāda to refer to such a classification.

But the later commentators are always eager to emphasise the syncretism of the Nyāya and the Vaiśeṣika schools. They think that it is their duty to show that the Nyāya and the Vaiśeṣika generally belong to the same tradition and also subscribe mostly to common views. Thus, as Śrīdhara notes, a simple answer to the question why this classification is not mentioned by Praśastapāda is that it is obviously accepted in the Vaiśeṣika system also, because it has been already admitted by the allied system (*samāna tantra*).[32] But, as we have already seen, neither Gautama nor Vātsyāyana refers to any such classification. It is rather a late development.

But others are not satisfied with such a simple explanation. They explain the definition taking the various qualifications in different combinations.[33] The statement giving the characteristics of a valid mark is not a single statement. Actually there are three statements referring to the three forms of mark. Thus, the first two, namely, 'that which is present in the *pakṣa*' and that which is present in the *sapakṣa*, refer to only-positive mark. Again, the first and the third characteristics, namely, 'that which is present in the *pakṣa*' and that which is never present in the *vipakṣa*', refer to the only-negative mark. All the three characteristics taken together refer to the mark which is positive-negative.

Of course, it may be objected that in that case we do not have a general definition of a valid mark. To this, it is answered that there will be no difficulty, because a general definition would be available by implication. If there be a *sādhya*, there must be a *sādhana*. Thus we can have a general definition that whatever is a capable means for establishing a thesis is a valid mark. We have a similar case in the general definition of *pramāṇa*. The different *pramāṇas* are differently defined referring to their special characteristics. But we can have a general definition of *pramāṇa* by implication, namely, that which reveals the object as it really is a *pramāṇa*.

Finally, Udayana also approves of this interpretation.[34] According to him also, there are actually three statements of characteristics referring to the three forms of inference under discussion. He also categorically states that the statement should not be taken as mentioning only the characteristics of a positive-negative mark. There is no doubt that the other two forms, the only-positive and the only-negative, are also valid according to the Vaiśeṣika tradition. He also gives an argument for his contention, though very briefly. While discussing the different types of inference-components (*avayava*), Praśastapāda says that a corroborative instance (*nidarśana*) may be of two kinds, based on similarity and based on dissimilarity. The second form of instance derives its validity from agreement in absence. It therefore shows that Praśastapāda also admits that pervasion (*vyāpti*) may also be established negatively. In other words, an only- negative mark also may be based on pervasion and as such, has to be accepted as valid.

In this connection, Udayana further notes that though only three characteristics have been mentioned, actually it cannot be said that a mark with the three alone leads to a correct inference, because it may be shown that even such a mark may not be capable of doing so. But it is also a fact that only the three have been mentioned and the other two, namely, absence of contradiction and absence of a counteracting mark, have been left out. According to him, the reason for not mentioning the two is that they are common to all the three forms of inference (under discussion). Only those three characteristics which are responsible for making the three forms of mark conclusive in each case have been mentioned. Thus, for example, the capability of an only-positive mark for leading to a correct inference lies in the fact that it is present only in *sapakṣas* and the capability of an only-negative mark for leading to a correct inference lies in the fact that it is never present in *vipakṣas*. Of course, an objection may be easily raised. If it be so, then, the first characteristic, presence in *pakṣa*, should also need not be mentioned, because it is common to all forms of inference. Udayana is aware of the objection and answers that in that case the mark will be without any basis at all (*nirāśraya*) and it would in fact become impossible to determine the nature of the mark. Nothing can be affirmed, nor can anything be denied, without an actual basis. Therefore, it is quite justified that only the three characteristics have been mentioned.

Process of Inference and Its Classification

After enumerating the essential characteristics of a valid mark and commenting that any mark lacking in only one or two of them would not lead to a valid knowledge of the inferable property, Praśastapāda very briefly describes the process of inference. He says:

"The process (of inference) is as follows: Wherever there is smoke there is fire; where there is no fire there is no smoke-a person who is well aware of this concomitance, when he has an absolutely certain perception of smoke, he recalls to his mind its concomitance (with fire), and after that is produced the definite knowledge of fire. Thus in all cases when one thing is invariably concomitant with another in point of time and place, it becomes a mark for the other."[35]

As commentators have pointed out a few points from this description may be noted. To be able to infer, a person must have already the knowledge of the concomitance (*samaya*) between the mark and the inferable property, and the concomitance is to be ascertained both positively and negatively. Secondly, he must make sure that he has a definite perception of the invariable mark and is not taking something else for the mark, e.g. in the inference of fire, he must be definite that he is perceiving smoke and not vapour (*vāṣpa*) or anything similar.[36] Actually, one perceives the mark, recalls its concomitance and immediately after acquires the knowledge of the inferable property. As is wellknown in later Nyāya, a further ascertainment or cognition in the form that the subject (*pakṣa*) possesses the mark which is concomitant with the inferable property is also admitted to be necessary for the production of inference. But Praśastapāda does not seem to subscribe to this view.

In fact, Śrīdhara has raised the question. He clearly says that in this description there is no reference to this additional knowledge technically known as *parāmarśa*. He comments further that this is alright, because such a cognition is not necessary. The knowledge of the inferable property may well be produced from the two factors, namely, perception, of the mark and recollection of the concomitance.[37]

It may be objected that if the knowledge of the inferable property is produced by a recollective cognition it would not be possible to relate the object inferred to a particular point of space. But it is necessary to do so, because it is found that after having the knowledge of an object through inference one proceeds in a definite direction to collect it. Śrīdhara says in answer that there will be no such difficulty because the relation of the object inferred with a specific point of space would be determined by the perception of the mark, i.e. the object would be inferred in that particular place only where the marks is actually observed. Smoke is perceived in the hill and therefore, fire would be inferred as present in the hill only.[38]

Śrīdhara has noted another objection also. As we shall see later, an inference generally consists of five steps or statements. The fourth step is called *upanaya* which makes sure that the mark as invariably concomitant with the object to be inferred is present in the subject. But if we accept the above description, this fourth step would become irrelevant. In answer, Śrīdhara says that it is not so, because *upanaya* has to be employed always in the case of inference for the sake of others as it would serve the purpose of pointing out the fact that the mark belongs to the subject, a fact not indicated by any other statement or inference-component.[39]

The other commentator Udayana however follows a totally different line of interpretation. According to him, Praśastapāda also follows the position as accepted in later Nyāya-Vaiśeṣika works, that is, for the production of inferential knowledge *parāmarśa* also is necessary.[40] Actually, in the process of inference, we must have three perceptions of the mark. First, the mark is perceived as located in the subject; secondly, it is perceived as having concomitance with the inferable property; and lastly, the mark as having concomitance is perceived as present in the subject. Udayana also argues that the perception of the mark and the recollection of concomitance only cannot lead to inference. For example, a person actually cognises smoke in the hill, but he fails to specify it as smoke and takes it simply as some object, and then accidentally he has the recollective awareness that smoke is concomitant with fire. Here we have both the first and the second cognitions of the mark, and hence, inferential knowledge should follow. But the fact is that it is not produced. The reason is that the third perception of the mark is absent here. Secondly, inference cannot be produced by the recollective cognition of the concomitance, because there the mark is not specifically revealed as the mark, but only as a certain object having concomitance with something else.

Udayana further argues that if *parāmarśa* is not accepted, the relevance of *upanaya* cannot in any way be defended. The knowledge of concomitance is not enough, it is also necessary to ascertain that the mark having concomitance is present in the subject. This purpose can be served only by *parāmarśa* and *upanaya* is necessary both in an inference for one's own self and an inference for the sake of others.[41]

Praśastapāda has specially remarked that one thing becomes an inferential mark for another when the two are invariably concomitant in time and place. The stock example is that of smoke and fire. Smoke accompanies fire always and everywhere. But the commentators explain that inference is possible on the basis of concomitance in either place or time. An instance of the first, as given by Śrīdhara, is the guarding of barley fields in Kashmir by persons in charge of gold is indicative of the fact that gold is being produced in the waterways in barley fields. Similarly, as an instance of concomitance in time, we have the singing of the morning songs and music in the houses of the *prāgjyotiṣa* which indicate that the king has woke up from sleep.[42] Other commentators also have given some typical examples.

Thus, briefly, the idea is that if one thing has invariable concomitance with another one can be inferred from the other. But, as we have already seen, Kaṇāda seems to have actually enumerated the cases where inference is possible.

Perhaps Praśastapāda himself and his commentators definitely apprehend that there may be a scope for his view being in contradiction with that of the Sūtrakāra. But this is not surely a desirable situation and ways for its avoidance have been suggested.

In fact, it is generally accepted that a reference to the *sūtra* enumerating the possible cases of inference has been made by Praśastapāda. Thus, after giving his own account of inference, he remarks that, in the *śāstra*, cases of inference with effect (*kārya*) etc. have been mentioned only for the purpose illustration (*nidarśana*) and not for that of specifying (*avadhāraṇa*); it is not meant that they are the only cases of inference.[43] Śāstra is obviously Kaṇāda's Vaiśeṣikaśāstra and all the major commentators agree on this point and quote the relevant *sūtra* from Kaṇāda's work. Why should it not be taken as an exhaustive enumeration? Praśastapāda says that some cases of inference may indeed be cited which cannot be included in any of these types. He gives three examples: The inference of the unseen Hotṛ from the utterance of the word *om* by the Adhvaryu, the rising of the moon leads to the inference of the swelling of the sea or the blooming of the lily, and in the autumn, clearness of water leads to the inference of the rise of the star Agastya.[44]

If the said *sūtra* is not an exhaustive enumeration, these cases of inference also should be admissible in Kaṇāda's view. But how? Praśastapāda answers that all additional cases are covered by the expression *asyedam*, which actually states the general ground of inference, namely, that one must have concomitance with the other. In other words, the *sūtra* may be said to have two parts: one is *asyedam* stating a general rule and the other, the rest, giving some illustrations.

The above is how the position of Praśastapāda is generally interpreted. According to both Udayana and Śrīdhara, his contention is that the effect etc. are only illustrations. Śrīdhara takes particular care to explain why the additional cases cited by Praśastapāda do not come under any of the types mentioned by Kaṇāda. For example, referring to the first example of Praśastapāda, he remarks that it is laid down that the Adhvaryu priest should repeat *om* to the Hotṛ priest and to no one else. Thus when one who is aware of this rule hears *om* repeated by the Adhvaryu, one infers the presence of the Hotṛ who may be sitting behind the walls and not visible. Here the Adhvaryu is neither the case, nor the effect, nor conjunct, nor the contradictory, nor the inherent, of the Hotṛ.[45]

At the first instance Vyomaśiva also agrees with the above and gives the general interpretation. But he also specially records that this view is not unanimous and there are some who think that the *sūtra* in question actually specifies the cases of inference. The remarks of Praśastapāda are differently explained by them.[46]

It is contended that Praśastapāda's real implication is that the view, namely, the reference to effect etc. is only illustrative since additional cases of inference are possible, represents the opponent's view, which does not stand logically. All the three cases supposed to be not covered by Kaṇāda's enumeration can be in fact shown to be covered by it. Thus, the Adhvaryu utters the particular word only when the Hotṛ is present nearby never otherwise, and this indicates that there is a causal relation between the two facts, namely, the presence of the Hotṛ and the utterance of *om*. Similarly a causal relation between the rising of the moon and the swelling of the sea is established on the basis of agreement in presence and agreement in absence. The one is found only when the other is present and when the other is absent the one is also absent. Here also the cause, the moon hidden by the clouds, in inferred from the effect, the swelling of the sea. The same applies to the blooming of the lily and the rising of the moon. It can also be explained as a case of the conjunct, because the moon becomes conjoined with the lily through its rays and makes it bloom. The clearness of water on the rise of the star Agastya also may be understood in the same way.[47]

Vyomaśiva concludes with the comment that the task of judging the relative merits and demerits of the alternatives be best left to the experts.[48]

Śaṅkara Miśra's view is in conformity with the generally interpreted position of Praśastapāda. But he arrives at the conclusion in a different way, with a rather far-fetched explanation. He also contends that this interpretation is suggested by Kaṇāda himself in the *sūtra* immediately following the one discussed above (i.e. 9.2.2). The term *avayavāt* there is a case of *lyablope pañcamī* and taking *avayava* in the sense of one of the essential components of the inferential process, namely, an example (*udāharana*), we should take it as equivalent to *udāharaṇam anurudhya*, i.e. with a view to providing an example. Thus, as clarified by the present *sutra* (9.2.2), Kaṇāda's implication is that *asyedam* gives the general condition for legitimate inference and the reference to the causal relation is by way of illustration.

While discussing the nature of inferential relation (*anumānāṅga-sambandha*) in the NVTT, Vācaspati Miśra objects to the Vaiśeṣika view of fourfold relation. Of the two *sūtras* under discussion, the former (9.2.1) is quoted and criticised by him.[49] The idea is as follows. The first part *asyedam* states that if one thing has a relation with another, one may be an inferential mark for the other. If it is meant that the relation should be invariable, it would be sufficient to state this part only. Wherever there is an invariable relation between two, inference of one from the other is permissible. It does not matter whether it is a case of the conjunct, the inherent or something else. If it is a case of valid inference it would naturally be covered by the first part. That is, the second part of the *sūtra* becomes redundant. If, on the other hand, it is admitted that the first part speaks of only a relation and thus it may be applicable even to fallacious cases, and hence, cases of valid inference are enumerated by the second part, it would be sufficient to state only this part, i.e. inference of one from the other is legitimate only in these cases and nowhere else. It does not matter whether or not there is a relation between the two, for all relations do not lead to inference. That is, the first part of the *sutra* becomes redundant.

Moreover, quoting examples of each, Vācaspati Miśra also takes exception to the cases of inference based on opposition as noted by Kaṇāda. His contention is that when there is really opposition between two, one is not an inferential mark for the other; actually, one negates the other. In the *Pariśuddhi*, Udayana makes no comment, but in the *Kiraṇāvalī* (as we have noted above) he clearly refers to Vācaspati's objection without naming him and replies that one or two examples of opposition may be unsatisfactory, but it does not mean that there is no genuine example of opposition. Simply from the non-existence of one the existence of another cannot be invariably ascertained, it is possible only when there is opposition between the two. He also formulates a definition of opposition and argues that inferences based on it are indeed possible.[50]

We have already seen that Kaṇāda himself does not give any clear indication as to the classification of inference. But Praśastapāda is definite in this respect and says that inference is of two kinds, *dṛṣṭa* and *sāmānyato dṛṣṭta*. Describing them, he says :

"A *dṛṣṭa* inference is that in which the *prasiddha*, that which is already known (as concomitant with the mark), and the sādhya, whose presence has to be proved, belong absolutely to the same class. As for instance, when one has seen the dewlap only in the body of a cow, whenever, on any subsequent occasion, he happens to see the dewlap, he infers the existence of the cow.[51]

"When however the *prasiddha* and the *sādhya* belong to absolutely different classes, the inference follows only from the concomitance of the general property of the mark with the general property of the object to be inferred; and this inference is called the *sāmānyato dṛṣṭa*. As for instance, having found that the activity of persons like the farmer, the trader and the servants of the king invariably leads to certain results, we infer the fact that, in the case of persons observing the rites of their respective castes and orders also, the activity which is not found to have any visible result, must produce definite results."[52]

In the first case a person has observed that the dewlap is present only in a certain animal which is characterised by the universal of cowness (i.e. an individual cow) and then finding only the dewlap in some other place he infers the presence of a certain animal which also is characterised by the universal of cowness (i.e. another individual cow). Thus there is identity between the two, namely, the thing observed earlier and the thing inferred later. That is why it is called *dṛṣṭa*, seen, as observed earlier. It is thus clearly identical with Gautama's *pūrvavat* according to the second interpretation of Vātsyāyana.[53] Two objects were previously perceived as related with each other. Later on, an object similar to one of them is perceived somewhere else and this leads to the inference there of another object similar to the other. Smoke and fire are perceived in the kitchen etc. as related to each other. The same kind of smoke is perceived in the hill and the same kind of fire is inferred in the hill.

In the second case, we have the inference of unseen result. Every action leads to some result as it is generally observed in the case of a peasant, a merchant or a royal officer. Thus, the actions of those following the duties prescribed for the castes and orders also must yield some result. But since they do not exert themselves for obtaining any seen or ordinary result, the result of their actions must be unseen. Here also we have actually two steps. The inference first proves the result generally and then, it is proved specifically. We have already pointed out that *sāmānyato dṛṣṭa* is clearly mentioned by Gautama as a distinct form of inference and Vātsyāyana has interpreted it in two ways.[54] That there is some basic similarity in the views of Praśastapāda and Vātsyāyana in this regard is beyond doubt. In the first interpretation, the example given is the inference of the sun's movement which is imperceptible - a case where there is no possibility of ascertaining by direct observation the invariable relation between the mark and the inferable property. In the second interpretation also it is clearly stated that in such an inference the invariable relation cannot be known directly and the example given is the inference of the self from its specific qualities. As commentators point out here also two steps are involved. First, it is proved generally that the specific qualities have a substance as their locus, and then, it is proved specifically that it cannot be anything other than the self.

The author of the *Vyomavatī* explains the example of the second type in a somewhat different way.[55] Thus, it may be asked, what kind of result does this inference try to prove- the seen or the unseen? It is not the seen, because it would be proving the proved (*siddhasādhana*). No one disputes the fact that every action produces some seen result. Then the inference itself would be useless. Of course, it may be argued that the question of proving a seen result does not arise here, because Praśastapāda clearly adds that in the case under consideration the agents do not desire any seen result. In other words, the inference is put forward to prove only some unseen result. But that is also not possible, because it is not possible to cite any instance corroborating the concomitance between the mark and the inferable property. We invariably find that an action is accompanied by a seen result, and not by an unseen one. The reason would also suffer from the fallacy of contradiction (*viruddha*), because the concomitance establishes a seen result whereas the mark tries to prove an unseen result.

In answer, the commentator says that the purpose of the inference is to prove some result in general without having any specific reference to the actual nature of the result. Thus, both in the cases of the peasant etc. and the followers of caste etc., it is generally established that the agents desire some result. So there is neither a lack of corroborative instance nor contradiction. Subsequently the inference points to the result with its specific nature (i.e. the unseen). The commentator also argues that such is the case with every inference. An inference establishes first the *sādhya* in general, which subsequently brings in or rests on the specific. If this position is not accepted, inference cannot be at all admitted as a source of valid knowledge.[56]

Concluding his discussion on the inferential process Praśastapāda says that the division of *pramāṇa* and its result in the case of inference may be represented in two ways. First, the instrument of knowledge is the perception of a mark, the result is the knowledge of the inferable object, the object of knowledge is the inferable object itself and the knower is the self. Of course, it may be asked, how can the perception of the mark be the cause for the ascertainment of the inferable property as the object of knowledge in each case is different and thus it is not possible to show the co-existence between the cause and the effect? All the commentators refer to this objection and give the same answer, namely, with reference to the appearance of knowledge there may be difference as regards the object but since the knowledge of the mark acts as *vyāpāra* for the production of the knowledge of *sādhya*, with reference to this *vyāpāra*, it may be said to have as object also the *sādhya*.[57]

In the second alternative, Praśastapāda says that (in the inference of fire from smoke) the knowledge of fire itself may be considered the instrument of knowledge and the result may be taken to be its specific ascertainment as having the character of either the good (*guṇa*) or the bad (*doṣa*) or the indifferent (*madhyastha*). As all the commentators agree, these ascertainments represent what is known in Nyāya terminology as *upādana-buddhi*, *hāna-buddhi* and *upekṣābuddhi*. In other words, after ascertaining the presence of fire from smoke, one ascertains either that it is a means for pleasure or that it is a means for suffering or that it is a means for neither.[58]

We have already discussed the classification of inference made by Praśastapāda on one principle. But Praśastapāda has also admitted the classification of inference adopting a different principle. He has clearly spoken of two classes of inference, *svārtha* or for one's own self and *parārtha* or for the sake of others.[59] As is wellknown, this classification has been admitted by all the systems of Indian philosophy in spite of mutual differences on various points regarding its nature.

However, it is difficult to conclude categorically which system is originally responsible for introducing this classification. It is certain that Kaṇāda does not speak of any such classification. Gautama also does not explicitly refer to it, although he discusses in details the nature of *avayava*, which is mentioned in the first *sūtra* as a separate category but is intrinsically related to the form known as *parārtha*. Still, there is no doubt that this classification was in vogue even at an early period. In fact, it has been approved, discussed and illustrated by the later followers of the different systems with great care and enthusiasm.

In all probability, the classification was introduced either by the Buddhists or the Vaiśeṣikas, though it is difficult to form any definite conclusion. One of the oldest texts in which we come across this division is Diṅnāga's *Pramāṇa -Samuccaya*, which presents us with well-formulated definitions of both the forms.[60] However, his treatment of the Vaiśeṣikas as the major opponent in the chapter on *parārtha* inference indicates that it actually formed the subject of a very old controversy. Sucarita Miśra, a later Mīmāṃsaka of the Bhāṭṭa school, explicitly mentions that *parārtha* inference is a Buddhist supposition. It is significant in the sense that it points to the fact that among the ancients the Buddhists were the ardent advocate of this classification of inference.

From the writings of some of the commentators of the various school, it is also clear that some philosophers are not ready to accept this classification. Śrīdhara, for example, briefly discusses the problem.[61] The opponent may argue that the very idea of a *parārtha* inference is an absurdity. Even in the case of a so-called *parārtha* inference there is no difference in the inferential process and the knowledge is acquired by the hearer himself and not by anybody else. Just as sometimes one may oneself perceive a mark having invariable concomitance and ascertain the presence of the inferable property, so also sometimes one may oneself ascertain a valid mark through the statement of another person and come to know of the presence of the inferable property. It cannot be argued that a *parārtha* inference is so called on the ground that is such a case there is a statement made for the benefit of others. When one communicates one's own perceptual cognition to somebody else for his benefit, it is not recognised as a *parārtha* perception on a similar ground.

In answer, it is pointed out that it is true that the knowledge in the case of such an inference also pertains to the hearer himself. Still it is called *parārtha*, because the hearer becomes aware of a mark having invariable concomitance - which he himself does not ascertain - through the words of somebody else who has already ascertained it, and subsequently he is led to the inference. The basis of the inference is thus furnished by a different person. With regard to the hearer, it is a *svārtha* inference, but with regard to the speaker, it is a *parārtha* inference. As to the case of the communication of a piece of perceptual cognition, there is no question of similar admission, because there the words of the speaker do not help the hearer to have any subsequent perceptual cognition.

Giving the definition of a *parārtha* inference, Praśastapāda says that it consists in expounding a conclusion ascertained by one's own self by means of a statement having five components (*avayava*). Explaining the definition, Śrīdhara says that one oneself ascertains the presence of a mark which has invariable concomitance with the inferable property and infers its presence. To communicate it to others one has to employ a statement which is capable of doing so. This statement consists of five component sentences and taken together they can produce the inferential knowledge in the others. The five component sentences point to the presence of the five essential characteristics of a mark which account for its validity and invariable concomitance with the inferable property. When the other person acquires the knowledge of such a mark through the statement he infers the presence of *sadhya*. The knowledge of the *sādhya* is not acquired through the statement, because it is not a form of verbal knowledge. Thus, in fact, a *parārtha* inference means the employment of a statement which speaks of a mark having invariable concomitance with the *sādhya*.[62]

Praśastapāda has not only accepted *parārtha* inference, but has also pointed out its special importance. According to him, one's own conclusion may be established through such an inference to three kinds of people, namely, one who has a doubt, one who has a false notion, and one who is not qualified enough.[63] The idea is that when a thesis is shown to be established through the five components of a *parārtha* inference it is established beyond doubt.

It may be noted that this idea also occurs in Vātsyāyana's commentary on the NS. He further emphasizes the position by maintaining that the special efficacy of the components lies in the fact that at the root of each component there is a specific *pramāṇa*. Thus, in the introduction to the first *sūtra* of Gautama, he comments:

"Each of the five propositions with which the desired thesis is conclusively established is called an inference-component (*avayava*) in relation to their totality. The four *pramāṇas* are collectively present (i.e. underlie) in these five. The preliminary statement of the thesis (*pratijñā*) is verbal testimony (*āgama*). The statement of the mark (*hetu*) is inference (*anumāna*). The exemplification (*udāharaṇa*) is perception (*pratyakṣa*). The application (*upanaya*) is comparison (*upamāna*). The demonstration of the capability of all of them to combine for the sake of establishing one central thesis is the conclusion (*nigamana*). This is *nyāya* par excellence."

As Uddyotakara points out the combination of the five components is called *nyāya* par excellence, because truth ascertained by them is beyond the scope of controversy and it is convincing for ever a person who may be under doubt, because it amounts to be ascertained jointly by all the four instruments of valid knowledge. Vātsyāyana points out further that without this *nyāya* no form of debate for the ascertainment of truth can proceed. This *nyāya* is the main instrument in the hands of the philosophers in their quest for the final conclusion. Of course, the Vaiśeṣikas admit only two *pramāṇas*, perception and inference, and any other form is included in inference. Still, Praśastapāda does not deny the importance of a *parārtha* inference.

The Five Inference-Components

Like Gautama, Praśastapāda also speaks of five components, though the names given to each and also their nature to some extent vary. Thus, according to Praśastapāda, the components are: statement of thesis (*pratijñā*), the statement of mark (*apadeśa*), the instance (*nidarśana*), the application (*anusandhāna*) and reiteration (*pratyāmnāya*).[64] He discusses the nature of each in details.

An object which is sought to be established as the locus of some property is called the subject (*anumeya* = *pakṣa*). The first component is a mere statement of the subject. Its only purpose is to communicate what one is going to prove. There is no reference to the ground or anything else. For example, the statement 'air is a substance.'[65]

As against this, the Buddhists argue that a mere statement of the thesis without any reference to the ground or the mark does not in any way contribute to the proving of what is to be proved, and as such, it does not deserve to be mentioned as a component. In fact, the statement of the mark actually is capable of indicating what is going to be proved and simply making a statement of an object qualified by a property does not make any sense. Refuting the contention the Vaiśeṣikas argue that a specific mark is capable of establishing a specific thesis. Therefore, it is necessary, before one puts forward a mark, to state precisely the conclusion one is trying to establish by that mark. If there is no preliminary statement of thesis, the subsequent statements of the mark etc. would become useless, because they would have nothing to hold on to, i.e. something in respect of which they may be operative.[66]

The definition of *pratijñā* is thus partly in agreement with the one given by Gautama, who also defines it as the specific mention of what is sought to be proved.[67] But there is an important difference between the two definitions in the fact that Praśastapāda adds a further qualification, namely, the statement must not be contradicted by perception, inference, verbal testimony, one's own doctrine and one's own statement.

An example of the first is: Fire is not hot. Since fire is proved to be hot by tactual perception one cannot put forward a thesis in such a form. Śrīdhara points out why such a formulation is considered faulty. The error (*doṣa*) here does not pertain to the subject, because the object presented as the subject always retains its own character. The error cannot also pertain to the mark, because the mark is always capable of proving its own object, i.e. the thing with which it has invariable concomitance. No mark can prove what lies beyond its scope. So the error must pertain to the propounder of the argument, because it is he who brings forward the mark for proving something which does not constitutes its proper object.[68]

An example of the second is: *ākāśa* is dense. According to the Vaiśeṣika, *ākāśa* is not perceptible and it is proved as a separate substance by an inference. The inference which proves its existence also proves it to be eternal and partless. Thus, if one admits *ākāśa* and wants to prove that it is dense or has its component parts tightly held together goes against the very basic inference.[69]

An example of the third is: wine is a thing which can be drunk by a Brahmin. The implication is that even if a Brahmin drinks wine he will not acquire any sin. The corroborative instance in this case would be milk, because, the drinking of milk is not sinful. But how is this fact known? The answer is that it is known from *śruti*, *smṛti* and *āgama*. But the same scriptural statement which establishes that there is no sin in drinking milk also proves that there is sin in drinking wine. Thus the validity of the instance is disproved and ṣuch a thesis cannot be put forward.[70]

An example of the fourth occurs when a follower of the Vaiśeṣika offers the thesis that an effect is pre-existing. That the effect is pre-existing in the cause is a thesis held by the Sāṃkhya and the Vaiśeṣika has refuted it, his own contention being that before production an effect is non-existing .If he offers a thesis like the above it would be in contradiction with his own doctrine.[71]

An example of the fifth or the last is: words are not capable of conveying any meaning. In other words, it is a case of self-contradiction. If the speaker really believes that words do not convey any meaning he should not make a statement like this to express his opinion. On the other hand, if he makes the statement to convey his own conclusion he cannot but accept that words do convey meaning.[72]

It is interesting to note that this definition of Praśastapāda has got much similarity with the one as presented in the Buddhists tradition. In the *Nyāyabindu*, we find a definition which most probably comes originally from Dinnāga mentioned and elaborated by Dharmakīrti.[73] There also among the various conditions laid down one is that in spite of fulfilling the other conditions a thesis is not to be regarded as a thesis if it is contradicted by perception, inference, general usage (*prasiddhi*) or one's own statement. An example of the first is: sound is inaudible. The audibility of sound is, in fact, proved by perception. An example of the second is: the jar is eternal. That the jar is noneternal is a fact proved by inference. Whatever is a product is found to be noneternal. The jar also is a product. How can it be eternal? An example of the third is: The hare-marked (*śaśin*) is not denoted by the word 'moon'. It is established by general usage that the hare-marked object shining in the sky is denoted by the word 'moon'. Hence the statement becomes contradicted. An example of the fourth is: inference is not a *pramāṇa*. According to the Buddhists, verbal testimony is not a separate *pramāṇa*, but it is included in inference. If the speaker really intends that his words should convey any meaning he has to accept that inference is a *pramāṇa*. On the other hand, if he really thinks that inference has no validity he should not make the statement itself.

Praśastapāda has stated the second component explicitly. It is a statement of the inferential mark. A valid mark is one which is present in the *pakṣa* and also the *sapakṣas* and is absent from all the *vipakṣas*. The statement of such a mark is the second component. For example, in the inference that air is a substance: because it has action and because it has qualities. Action and qualities are present in air, and also in most of the other substances, qualities being present in all but action being so in only some of them and lastly, both of them are absent from whatever is not a substance. Therefore, the statement of these two marks constitute the second component.[74]

Coming to the third component, Praśastapāda says that it may be of two kinds, based on similarity and based on dissimilarity. The purpose of mentioning an instance is to show clearly that there is some concrete case where the concomitance is actually present and can be verified. If an instance shows, positively, that the presence of the mark is invariably, accompanied by the presence of the inferable property, it would be of the first kind. For example, in the inference already mentioned, the statement: whatever is found to have action is found to be a substance, just as, an arrow. If the instance shows, negatively, that the absence of the inferable property is invariably accompanied by the absence of the mark, it would be of the second kind. For example, in the same inference, the statement: whatever is not a substance is found not to have any action, just as, the universal of *sattā*.[75]

Although the concept of fallacious mark (*hetvābhāsa*) is common to all the systems of Indian philosophy, the concept of fallacious instance is not so, being most probably a later development and advocated by only a few systems. Praśastapāda mentions twelve kinds of fallacious instance, six in the case of one based on similarity and six in the case of one based on dissimilarity.

For example, one puts forward the inference that sound is eternal, because it is immaterial (*amūrta*). If one offers as the third component the statement that whatever is found to be immaterial is eternal, for example, an atom, it would be a case of *liṅgāsiddha*. Here the mark immateriality is not present in the instance cited, because an atom must come from any of the four material substances. If, again, one offers action as the instance it would be a case of *anumeyāsiddha*, because the inferable property, eternality, is not present in it. Every action is non-eternal. Thirdly, if a jar is offered as the instance it would be a case of *ubhayāsiddha*, because neither the inferable property nor the mark, is present in it. A jar is both non-eternal and material. Fourthly, if darkness is offered as the instance it would be a case of *āśrayāsiddha*, because, in reality, there is nothing called darkness. How can the concomitance be verified with the help of something which does not exit? Fifthly, if only the sky (*ambara*) is offered as an instance, but there is no statement of the concomitance, it would be a case of *ananugata*. Both the inferable property and the mark are present in the instance, still it would be fallacious because of incompleteness. It is not sufficient to mention only the instance, it is also necessary to state the general form of concomitance involving the inferable property and the mark. Otherwise one would not have any idea as to the co-existence of which properties is being established and in fact, the instance itself would become useless. Thus, in this case, the proper statement should have been that whatever is immaterial is eternal, for example, the sky. Lastly, if one states the concomitance in a reverse form, namely, whatever is a substance is found to have action it would be a case of viparītānugata. There is invariable concomitance between the presence of action and being a substance, but not *vice-versa*. In this component the pervaded (*vyāpya*) and the pervader (*vyāpaka*) must be mentioned in their correct order; otherwise there will be no establishment of the concomitance and the inference itself may not succeed.[76]

Similarly, six examples of fallacious instance based on dissimilarity also are mentioned. For example, in the same inference, if action is cited as an instance to establish the concomitance that whatever is non-eternal is material it would be a case of *liṅgavyāvṛtta*. Because action may be non-eternal but it is also immaterial. If, again, an atom is offered as an instance, it would be a case of *anumeyavyāvṛtta*, because an atom may be material, but it is also eternal. If *ākāśa* is offered as an instance it would be a case of *ubhayavyāvṛtta*, because *ākāśa* is both eternal and immaterial. If darkness is offered as an instance, it would be a case of *āśrayāsiddha*, because nothing called darkness exists in reality. If such a thing does not exists at all how can it prove that there the absence of *sadhya* is accompanied by the absence of *sādhana*. If simply the jar is mentioned as an instance, but there is no statement of the concomitance that whatever is non-eternal is material, it would be a case of *avyāvṛtta*. Although both non-eternality and materiality are present in the jar, it is not sufficient to mention the jar only, because without a specific mention of the mark and the inferable property it is not possible to convince one of the intended concomitance. Lastly, if it is only stated that whatever is without an action is not a substance it would be a case of *viparītavyavṛtta*. Positively, the inferable, property is the pervader and the mark is the pervaded. Negatively, the absence of inferable property is the pervaded and the absence of the mark is the pervader. They have to be stated in their proper order. If it is stated that whatever is not a substance is not a locus of action, it would be possible to establish concomitance. But if the statement is made in a reverse order that whatever is without an action is not a substance, it becomes impossible to speak of concomitance, because *ākāśa* is without any action, but it is still a substance.[77]

It appears that in this case also Praśastapāda is following a tradition different from that of its ally, the Nyāya. In the Buddhist to tradition, all the authors assign an important position to the discussion of fallacious instances and it is easy to see that the views of Praśastapāda and the Buddhists have a close similarity, the names and the examples given being almost identical in both. For example, in the *Nyāyapraveśa*, attributed to Diṅnāga, there are mentioned, in all, ten types of fallacious instances, five in the case of similarity and five in the case of dissimilarity. But since the type called *ubhayāsiddha* is further classified into two sub-types, there also we have really twelve types. The account and classification given by Praśastapāda and Diṅnāga are identical. Though there is a slight difference in the names, it is not of any material importance. Dharmakīrti also gives a closely similar account of fallacious instances in the *Nyāyabindu*. Most of the names and example given again are the same. In the Sāṃkhya tradition, Māthara seems to be a follower of Praśastapāda. However, he recognises a total of ten types, because he does not accept *aśrayāsiddha* as a separate form.

A good discussion of fallacious instances is available in the Jaina tradition also. Here Siddhasena is the first to give an account of such instances. He does not specifically mention the total number of the types, but seems to maintain that there are eighteen types, nine belonging to each group. Māṇikyanandin summarises all the earlier traditions and recognises only eight types. He also replaces some old illustrations by new ones. Vādidevasūri follows him on the question of illustrations, but literally accepts Dharmakīrti's terminology etc. In some of his illustrations Dharmakīrti tries to belittle the traditions of rival philosophers. Vādidevasūri also does the same by deprecating Tathāgata Buddha in alternative illustrations. The great Jaina scholar Hemachandra also offers a detailed presentation of the topic. Though Dharmakīrti appears to be his model, he does not blindly follow him, but introduces a slight intelligent change. He rejects two types recognised by Dharmakīrti.

In the NM, while explaining the nature of the third inference-component (*udāharaṇa*), Jayanta sums up the discussion with the comment that since the nature of instances based on similarity and dissimilarity has been thoroughly discussed, it follows that if any instance is found to be lacking in any of the necessary property it would become a case of a fallacious instance. His account agrees with that of Diṅnāga in the *Nyāyapraveśa*. However, he also gives the justification for not mentioning them in the text of Gautama, like the fallacious reasons. Actually, the defects relating to the instances invariably occur because of some defects in the reason. So separate mention is not necessary. Jayanta himself has however mentioned them for the benefit of the students.[78]

Referring to the fourth component, application, Praśastapāda says that it consists in affirming the fact that the mark which has been ascertained in the instance to be accompanied by the inferable property is also present in the subject of inference itself. If it is simply stated that the mark is present in the subject it cannot indicate the presence of the inferable property in the subject, for in that state it is powerless. Therefore, it is necessary to show once again that the mark which is definitely concomitant with the inferable property is present in the subject. Thus, on the strength of concomitance and presence in the subject the mark becomes capable of proving the inferable property. The form of the application again may be two fold, positive and negative, namely, 'similarly air has action', and, 'similarly air is not without action'. It has been argued that if the fourth component is really so vital then, what is the necessity of the second component which simply states that the mark is present in the subject? To this, Śrīdhara answers that unless the mark is specifically mentioned at the outset no further progress in the inferential process would be possible. The instances etc. are all dependent upon the mark and therefore the second component indicating the mark is necessary, so that one may not be in the dark about what actually is being offered as the reason of inference.[79]

The last component, reiteration, is almost a re-statement of the first component, thesis. Both indicate the fact that the inferable property is present in the subject. But there is a vital difference between them. In the first the presence of the inferable property is not yet ascertained, but in the last it is so through the operation of the other subsequent components. For example, in the same inference, 'therefore, air must be a substance'[80]

In fact, there is some controversy regarding the justification for accepting both the first and the fifth as inference-components. Perhaps that is why Praśastapāda explains in some details why the fifth component is necessary and the inferential process comes to an end with it. His main point is that all the first four statements have meanings of their own and their capability is exhausted only at conveying them. But unless a sort of mutual connection is established among them and it is shown that they unitedly point to a single conclusion, there can be no inferential knowledge. This possibility is established by the last component and hence it cannot be rejected as unnecessary. Praśastapāda illustrates the whole process, mentioning specifically each of the five components, with the inference of noneternality in sound, a great bone of contention between the Nyāya-Vaiśeṣika and the Mīmāṃsaka.[81]

The texts of the different schools of Indian philosophy reveal that in spite of universal acceptance of *parārtha* inference, there is great divergence of opinion regarding the actual number of the steps or components. For example, according to Sāṃkhya, only three components are sufficient and they are the thesis, the reason and the instance. The Buddhists contend that only two components, the instance and the application, are necessary and in both *svārtha* and *parārtha* inferences the inferential cognition is produced by them. When the two statements - wherever there is smoke there is fire as in the kitchen and this mountain contains smoke - are made, one after the other, the person concerned easily concludes that here the fact sought to be established is nothing but fire and the ground is smoke. There are some who think that the statement of the thesis is necessary for indicating the nature of the inference, whether it is a formulation based on similarity or a formulation based on dissimilarity. The Jaina view seems to recognise in general the necessity of two components only. They reject the instance as unnecessary and argue that the purpose of the application and the conclusion are served by the thesis and the reason. But some Jaina logicians are of the opinion that the number of steps may not be fixed for one and all, but may be more or less according to the degree of intelligence or power of comprehension of the person concerned. The Mīmāṃsakas claim that there are only three components, which are either the thesis, the reason and the instance, or, the instance, the application and the conclusion. In the first alternative, the purpose of application is served by the reason and that of conclusion by the thesis. In the second alternative the purpose of reason is served by the application and that of thesis by the conclusion.[82]

However, in this regard the Nyāya and the Vaiśeṣika are completely united in contending that five components, neither more nor less, are essential. Against the criticism of all, specially the Buddhists, they strongly argue for the justification of each of the five component. Vātsyāyana is more explicit on this problem and time and again examines the effectiveness of the five components. Besides arguing that the conclusion is necessary for indicating the capability of mutually combining for a common purpose, Vātsyāyana maintains further that the purpose of the conclusion is to exclude the contrary possibility of the absence of the inferable property in the subject, after the *hetu-sādhya* relation between two properties perceived in an instance has been ascertained.[83]

Moreover, Vātsyāyana says that an inference consisting of five members is vital for a philosophical debate. He says:

"When the mark and the instance are thus correctly stated, the possibility of advancing any form of *jāti* and *nigrahasthāna*, resulting from a diversity of defects indicated on the basis of similarity and dissimilarity is excluded. Because one advancing a *jati* points to defects ignoring the *hetu-sādhya* relation between two properties perceived in an instance. When the *hetu-sādhya* relation between two properties is properly established, and when it is perceived in the instance cited, the property actually proving the inferable property-rather than mere similarity or mere dissimilarity-is taken as the mark."[84]

Classification of Fallacious Reasons.

The term for fallacious reason used by both Kaṇāda and Praśastapāda is the same, though rather uncommon, namely, *anapadeśa*. As is wellknown, the term generally used to indicate such reason is *hetvābhāsa*. The terms may be different, but there is no difference so far as the nature of them is concerned.

In the VS we have practically nothing in this regard. There is one *sūtra* which simply states that fallacious reasons are of three types, and two *sūtras* are added to illustrate them.[85] But from these brief remarks nothing definite is available and the commentators who belong to a much later period go by the traditions developed much later and there being no dependable hint explain them according to their own fancy. From Kaṅāda's *sūtra* this much only is clear that the fallacious reasons are called *aprasiddha*, *asan* and *sandigdha*.

According to Candrananda, the first one stands for what is later generally known as *viruddha*. For example, the inference, this animal is a horse, because it has horns. The reason here is contradictory because actual observation shows whatever animal has horns is not a horse. The second one occurs if the inferable property is not present in the subject, e.g. in the inference a hare has horns etc. The presence of horns is simply proved to be impossible in the case of a hare. But this is actually an example of what is well recognised in the Nyāya as the variety called *bādhita*. It is almost certain that this variety is not accepted in the Vaiśeṣika tradition. The third form is said to occur when the mark is accompanied by both the presence and absence of the inferable property in different instances. For example, in the inference, this animal is a cow, because it has horns. Horns are present in the cow and also in other animals like the buffalo etc. This corresponds to the most common form of what is later known as *savyabhicāra* or *anaikāntika*.[86]

Śaṅkara Miśra offers his own interpretation in a very different way. According to him, the term *aprasiddha* points to the type known as *viruddha* and *vyāpyatvāsidddha*. The term *asan* stands for the fallacies known as *svarūpāsiddha* and *siddhasādhana*. The term *sandigdha* lastly refers to the three forms of *anaikāntika*, all of which produce a doubt regarding the presence of the inferable property.[87]

While concluding his discussion on fallacious reasons, Śaṅkara Miśra refers to the view of Vṛttikāra who thinks that the particle *ca* used in the *sūtra* is in the sense of addition and the implication is that Kaṇāda also admits the two other forms known as *bādhita* and *satpratipakṣa* which are recognised by Gautama and thus the Vaiśeṣika and the Nyāya are unanimous on this point. But the commentator rightly points out it is difficult to accept such a conclusion, because

Praśastapāda has clearly stated that in Kaṇāda's view the fallacious reasons are only of three types, which definitely do not include the additional two.[88] All this proves only one point. The commentators have no idea of the actual implications of Kaṇāda. They are totally under the influence of views advocated much later and everyone freely runs away with his own imagination.

Praśastapāda's exposition is marked by clarity and precision. He states his views clearly and leaves little scope for speculation. His account is neither elaborate nor brief. He states the divisions clearly, gives the definitions and illustrations of each variety in a simple language. Incidentally, he also refers to and criticises the view of other who do not see eye to eye with him.

At the beginning of the section on inference, while enumerating the three essential characteristics of a valid mark, Praśastapāda remarks that a mark which is deficient in any one of the properties or in any two of the properties cannot lead to valid inference and hence the statement of such a mark becomes fallacious. Further, he quotes the relevant *sūtra* of Kaṇāda in support. According to Śrīdhara, a fallacious reason may be deficient either in only one property or in only two properties. But, according to the author of *Vyomavatī* and Udayana, a fallacious reason may also be deficient in all the three properties. Thus the former states that *sandigdha* is deficient in one property, *viruddha* in two properties and *asiddha* in either one or two or three properties. He also gives the examples for each.[89]

Although it is clear that Kaṇāda admits only three types of fallacious reason, commentators have still tried to offer their own interpretations. Udayana's view is similar to that of the Vṛttikāra, referred above.[90] Udayana thinks that a reason may be faulty due to a number of fallacies. The principle is to point out first the strongest one. The three fallacies specifically mentioned by Kaṇāda are stronger than *bādhita* and *satpratipakṣa*. Secondly, these two fallacies are common to all the three types of inference, namely, only-positive, only-negative and positive-negative. That is why the additional two are not separately mentioned by Kaṇāda. It is not that he does not admit them. In short, Kaṇāda also holds a view similar to that of Gautama. The author of *Vyomavatī* also shares the same opinion and briefly comments that these two are to be collected either by the term *aprasiddha* or due to the fact that they are accepted in the allied system (*samāna-tantra-nyāyena*).[91]

Śrīdhara, however, does not think that these two fallacies are accepted to be additional ones, but may be included in the three actually admitted. He discusses the views of others who admit them as separate ones, but finally rejects the view. Briefly, his arguments are as follows. In the case of *satpratipakṣa*, one cannot be restricted to a single alternative, (*ekānta*), rather there arises a scope for a doubt and hence, it may be included under *sandigdha* or *anaikāntika*. Again, in the case of *bādhita*, the subject is not at all a proper subject and therefore, the mark is not really present in the subject. It can be easily included in *asiddha*.[92]

Further, commenting on the three types of Kaṇāda, he says that *aprasiddha* stands for *viruddha* and *asādhāraṇa*, because in both cases the reason is not known to be accompanied by the inferable property. By the term *asan* we are to understand the fallacy of unproved (*asiddha*), because in this case the mark may be known to accompanied by the inferable property, but it is not actually present in the subject. The term *sandigdha* refers to *anaikāntika*. In this case, a mark may be present in the subject, but only leads to a doubt and not to an ascertainment, because it is accompanied by both the inferable property and its absence in different instances.[93]

We have already noted that so far as Praśastapāda's own view is concerned it is very clearly stated. He accepts all the three as mentioned by Kaṇāda, but also adds a fourth type of his own. Thus, according to him, the fourth types of fallacious reason are: the unproved (*asiddha*) the contradictory (*viruddha*), the doubtful (*sandigdha*) and the uncertain (*anadhyavasita*).

For the first no general definition is offered. The classification is given and each is defined and illustrated.[94] It is of four types. First, unproved for both the parties in a debate e.g. sound is non-eternal, because it is composed of parts. There may be controversy about the eternality or non-eternality of sound, but it is accepted by all that sound has no component parts. Secondly, unproved for either of the parties e.g. sound is non-eternal, because it is an effect. Sound is admitted to be an effect by the Vaiśeṣika, but it is not accepted to be so by the opponent, the Mīmāṃsaka. Thirdly, unproved as having a particular nature, e.g. when one mistakes vapour for smoke and tries to infer the presence of fire with its help. Fourthly, the case of unproved subject, e.g. darkness is an earth-substance, because it has black colour. There is no such substance as darkness and here the subject itself is unproved.

If a mark is present in the subject, but is absent from all *sapakṣas* and is moreover present in all *vipakṣas*, it will be a case of the contradictory, because it succeeds only in proving the opposite or the absence of the inferable property. For example, in a jungle, with reference to a cow hidden by bushes, one finds only the horns and puts forward the inference that this animal is a horse, because it has horns. Presence of horns is invariably related to the absence of a horse and therefore, the inference should prove just the opposite.

The doubtful is so called, because it gives rise to a doubt It is a mark which besides being present in the subject is also present in both *sapakṣas* and *vipakṣas*. For example, when one infers that an animal is a cow, because it has horns. Horns are present in cows and also in other animals like the buffalo etc. The mark, presence of horns, is thus accompanied by both the inferable property and its absence. In a particular case, therefore, the presence of the mark can at best give rise to a doubt: is it present here with the inferable property or with its absence? It cannot lead to an ascertainment of either. Hence, it becomes doubtful.

Lastly, the uncertain occurs if the mark is present only in the subject, but is absent from both *sapakṣas* and *vipakṣas*. It is illustrated by a peculiar Sāṃkhya view: an effect is existent (*sat*), because it is produced. It is true that an effect has production, but neither the things like *ākāśa* etc. nor hare's horns etc. have production. Thus the mark fails to lead to the ascertainment of any particular alternative and becomes a fallacious reason. According to Praśastapāda, it is admitted by Kaṇāda also, because it can be included in *aprasiddha*.

It is interesting to note that Praśastapāda has referred to and refuted certain views held by others on fallacious reasons.[95] When a property present both in *sapakṣas* and *vipakṣas* is offered as the mark and is found to be present in the subject, only a doubt regarding the inferable property may be produced, and it becomes a fallacious reason, called the doubtful. But there are some who speak of another variety of the doubtful. When two marks, both of equal strength, but establishing mutually opposed properties, are offered with reference to the same subject, there can be produced only a doubt regarding the inferable property. Such a case also represents a variety of the doubtful. For example, someone says that the mind is something concrete (*mūrta*), because it has movement, just like an arrow. But it may also be argued that the mind is not concrete, because it has no touch, just like *ākāśa*. Both the marks are valid. Whatever is found to have movement is also found to have a concrete form. Again, whatever is found to be without touch is also found to be without any concrete form. There are instances to corroborate both the concomitances. It cannot be said that both the marks establish their respective inferable properties, because they are opposed to each other and both of them cannot be present in a single substance. A substance cannot be both concrete and non-concrete. It can neither be claimed that both the marks are incapable of establishing the respective inferable properties because a substance must be either concrete or non-concrete as there is no third alternative. It is also not possible to show by any means that either of the marks is weaker than the other, both are equally capable. Thus, if one finds that movement and absence of touch are both found in the mind, one can at least have a doubt about the nature of the mind, whether it is concrete or non-concrete. As such, it is to be accepted as case of the fallacy known as the doubtful.

Before giving his final opinion, Praśastapāda refers to a view according to which such a case need not be accepted as a variety of the doubtful, but should rather be identified with the uncertain. As in the above illustration, the two properties, movement and absence of touch, are collectively present only in the mind and in no other substance. Other substances may have movement, but they are also characterised by touch. Again, some substances may be without touch, but they are also without movement. But both the properties are present together only in the mind and thus, they become a unique property of the mind, i.e. the subject. As we have already noted if a property belonging to the subject only is offered as a mark it becomes a fallacious reason called the uncertain.

Praśastapāda's own view is that a unique property cannot give rise to a doubt. Secondly, when both the marks are of equal strength, they fail, due to mutual opposition, to produce any ascertainment, but do not lead to a doubt. In fact, according to Praśastapāda, in such a case both the marks are not of equal strength because one of them becomes weaker being contradicted by the scripture (*āgama*). For example, in the above illustration, the thesis that the mind is not concrete is contradicted by Kaṇāda's statement that since there is no simultaneous production of cognitions the mind must be of an atomic magnitude (i.e. concrete). In other words, this so called variety of the doubtful is covered by the fallacious presentation of the thesis.[96]

It appears that some were not inclined to accept the uncertain as a separate variety. The contention was that, just like a common property, a unique property also might produce a doubt. Hence it should rather be called the doubtful. Praśastapāda however does not accept the view that a unique property also can cause a doubt. A doubt can be caused only by a common property, because it is found to be present along with two specific properties in different instances, and hence when it is found present in some object it leads to the recollection of the two opposite characteristics and as a result, two alternatives are presented and there is a doubt. If a unique property is accepted to be the cause of a doubt, innumerable doubts regarding all the categories will be produced continuously, because each and every object has a specific property of its own.[97]

NOTES & REFERENCES

1. AS, 1., 2.1-12
2. Cf. Vātsyāyana's interpretation of the term *ānvīlkṣikī*, NS, 1.1.1.
3. For a discussion of the question, see Debiprasad Chattapadhyaya, *What is Living and What is Dead in Indian Philosophy*, pp. 247 ff.
4. VS, 10.1.3.
5. For *liṅga*, which is by far the most numerous, see VS, 1.2.17, 2.1.8, 3.1.19, 5.2.9. etc. For hetu, see VS, 3.1.2, 3.1.7., 9.2.4 and 10.1.2.
6. VS, 9.2.4.
7. VS, 3.1.14.
8. See, for example, Śrīdhara's explanation of the term *prasiddha* in Praśastapāda's definition of *saṃśaya* and *sāmānyato-dṛṣṭa* inference.
9. VS, 3.1.9. and 9.2.1.
10. The examples are generally taken from *Upaskāra*.
11. VS, 3.1.11-13 and *Upaskāra* thereon.
12. See VS, 2.1.8., 2.1.10., 2.1.15 and 3.2.6.
13. NS, 1.1.5.
14. VS, 2.1.16 and 3.2.7.
15. VS, 2.1.17 and 2.1.27.
16. VS, 2.1.24-27. See also *Upaskāra* on 2.1.27.
17. On NS, 1.1.5.
18. NS, 3.2.39.
19. PPbh, p. 476.
20. *Vyomavatī*, p.147.
21. NK, pp. 476- 447.
22. Ibid, p.477. Cf. also NM, pt. I. p.21.
23. Ibid.
24. *Kiraṇāvalī*, p. 545.
25. PPbh, pp. 478-479.
26. See, for example, Diṅnāga's view quoted in NVTT, pp. 319.-320.
27. For a comparative discussion, see Sukhlalji Sanghvi, ASILM, pp. 87ff.
28. *Vyomavatī*, pp. 149 f.
29. NK, pp. 482-485.
30. On NS, 1.1.5.

31. *Vyomavatī*, pp. 151-152, NK, pp. 486 ff.
32. NK, p. 489.
33. *Vyomavatī*, p.153, NK, p. 489.
34. *Kiraṇāvalī*, pp. 550 f.
35. PPbh, p. 491.
36. NK, p. 491. See also *Vyomavatī*, p. 155.
37. Ibid.
38. Ibid.
39. Ibid, p. 492.
40. *Kiraṇāvalī*, p. 554,
41. Ibid, p. 556.
42. NK, p. 503.
43. PPbh, p. 503.
44. Ibid, pp. 504-505.
45. NK, pp. 504-505.
46. *Vyomavatī*, p 159.
47. Ibid.
48. Ibid, p 160.
49. NVTT, pp. 308-309. See also NV, p. 302.
50. Ibid.
51. PPbh, p. 507.
52. Ibid, pp. 508-509.
53. On NS 1.1.5.
54. Ibid.
55. *Vyomavatī*, p. 161.
56. Ibid.
57. PPbh, p. 509.
58. Ibid, p. 510.
59. PPbh, pp. 510, 620.
60. In fact, in *Pramāṇasamuccaya*, the second and the third chapters are devoted to the treatment of the two forms.
61. NK, p. 564. See also NM, pt. II, p. 130.
62. NK, pp. 558-559.
63. PPbh, p. 560.

64. PPbh, p. 565.
65. Ibid, pp. 565-566.
66. NK, pp. 566-567.
67. NS, 1.1.33.
68. PPbh, p. 570.
69. Ibid, p. 572.
70. Ibid.
71. Ibid, p. 573.
72. Ibid.
73. NB, chapter III.
74. PPbh, pp. 575-576.
75. Ibid, pp. 598-599.
76. Ibid, p. 600.
77. Ibid, p. 604.
78. ASILM, pp. 106 ff.
79. PPbh, pp. 606, 610.
80. Ibid, p. 611.
81. Ibid, pp. 611 ff.
82. ASILM, pp. 85 f.
83. On NS, 1.1.39.
84. Ibid.
85. VS, 3.1.15-17
86. On VS, 3.1.10-12
87. On VS, 3.1.15.
88. On VS, 3.1.17.
89. PPbh, pp. 480-481 and NK, thereon.
90. *Kiraṇāvalī*, pp. 548-550.
91. *Vyomavatī*, p. 154.
92. NK, p. 483.
93. Ibid, p. 490.
94. PPbh, pp. 577f.
95. Ibid, pp. 581 ff.
96. Ibid, p. 590.
97. Ibid, pp. 594ff.

Chapter Four

Other Forms

Praśastapāda has classified valid knowledge into different forms in his own way. In fact, in this classification, he differs from all the other systems of Indian philosophy. Of course, the two most important forms are perception and inference, which are accepted by all the systems excluding only the Cārvāka. They have accordingly been discussed elaborately and given due prominence. In the preceding chapter we have tried to give an idea of Praśastapāda's views on them. In this chapter we shall take up the remaining two forms, namely, recollective cognition (*smṛti*) and intuitional cognition (*ārṣa*). Further, we shall also discuss here how some other forms of knowledge which are accepted by other systems are not accepted as separate ones but are included mostly under inference in the Vaiśeṣika view.

Recollective Cognition

Praśastapāda's remarks on this form of knowledge are brief and also not very clear. Recollective cognition reveals past (*atīta*) object. Some object to this description on the ground that such cognition may have for its object even a thing present and moreover, sometimes inferential knowledge also reveals past objects. Thus the definition may be said to be either too narrow or too wide. In answer, the commentators point out that the term 'past' is to be taken in a secondary sense, meaning not something which was previously existing, but as something which was known earlier.[1] It has been also suggested that the term may also be taken in the sense of an object which is not present before the cogniser (*vyavahita*).[2] However, Praśastapāda himself has specified the nature of objects that may be concerned with a recollective cognition. Accordingly to the interpretation of the commentators, they are of three types, namely, perceived earlier, known through words earlier and inferred earlier.[3]

Praśastapāda has first mentioned the causes of such cognition. They are two, namely, a special form of conjunction between the self and the mind and impression (*saṃskāra*). The conjunction again is not capable of producing it by itself; it has to be aided by some other factors like the perception of a mark, desire and associated ideas etc.[4] The impression again may be produced by a distinct cognition, by repetition and by special regard (*ādara*). By distinct cognition is meant a cognition produced in respect of objects desirable and undesirable, but not an object to which one is indifferent. Cognitions only in respect of the first two types of objects are capable of producing impressions powerful enough to give rise to recollective cognition later. But a cognition related to the third type of object is not so; for example, one may walk a long way over the grass but may not remember the grass later. The grass is a kind of object which is neither to be desired nor to be avoided. Sometimes it happens that even a distinct cognition does not produce a sufficiently powerful impression as we find in the case of a chapter of the Veda read for the first time. Though one has read it carefully, one cannot remember it. But when there are repetitions one can remember it, which means that a powerful impression has been produced so that the chapter is fixed in memory. Again, sometimes when one comes across a strange object, the cognition produced may be so impressive that even though the object is seen only once, it may be remembered for all times to come.[5]

Finally, Praśastapāda has also mentioned some typical effects produced by a re-collective cognition. First, it may produce the knowledge of an inferable object, e.g. the recollective cognition of the invariable concomitance between smoke and fire leads to the knowledge of fire. Secondly, it may be the cause of desire. One has earlier derives pleasure from a particular object. Later one comes across the same object and recollects that a similar object produced pleasure earlier and then, one has a desire for obtaining the object. Similarly, it may also cause aversion. Earlier one has suffered pain through a particular object. Once again, one comes across a similar object and remembers the fact that it was a cause of pain. This recollection produces aversion in respect of the object.[6]

It is clear that Praśastapāda definitely considers recollection as a form of valid knowledge. But it is also a fact that except the Jaina no other system in Indian Philosophy has accepted it as *pramāṇa*. The acceptance of recollection as *pramāṇa* may no doubt give rise to some difficulties. The commentators have tried their best to explain away the anomaly and to show on what ground its validity is to be rejected. We shall examine the problem in details in the next chapter when we deal with the different forms of invalid knowledge.[7]

Intuitional Cognition

This form of valid cognition also is very briefly described by Praśastapāda. To sages who are the authors of the Veda, there is produced, due to contact between the self and the mind aided by the special merit acquired through learning, penance and deep meditation (*samādhi*), a form of intuitional knowledge which reveals the objects as they really are. It is produced in respect of objects past, present and future and also in respect of *dharma* and other imperceptible objects which may or may not be spoken of in the scriptures. Praśastapāda adds that this kind of knowledge is generally possible in the case of divine sages, but in some exceptional cases it may be possible for any ordinary person also, e.g. when a little girl says 'my heart tells me that my brother will come tomorrow'.[8]

Commentators have naturally tried to show that it is a distinct form of knowledge. There can be no question about its validity. It is not a form of doubt because it is not concerned with two alternatives. It is also not an error, because the brother is actually found to arrive next day and thus it conforms to fact.[9]

At least one commentator records an objection to considering it as a form of distinct cognition. It is argued that it should be regarded as perceptual, because though there is no function of an external sense-organ, still it is produced through the operation of the internal sense. A direct contact between the sense and the object known, i.e. the brother, may not be possible, but still some sort of indirect relation between the two may be conceived. In fact, for the perception of many of the categories the relation accepted is an indirect one.[10] In answer, it is pointed out that in the case of such knowledge the assumption of the function of a sense organ is not necessary. Only in the cases of some direct cognitions it is essential to admit of a contact between the object and the sense. But in the case of intuitional cognition the objects may be such that a relation between the two may not be at all possible. Besides, in respect of an external object the mind cannot operate unless it is assisted by an external sense. But in the case of such cognition the mind acts without any operation of an external sense. If someone asks, how do you derive the knowledge, the person concerned does not refer to any external sense, but simply says that his 'heart' provides the information. The question of including it in the inferential or the verbal variety does not arise, because it is produced without the knowledge of a mark and its invariable concomitance or words.[11]

In the concluding part of his discussion an valid forms of knowledge Praśastapāda argues that the knowledge of persons with occult powers (*siddhadarśana*) or occult cognition should not be regarded as a distinct form. A person may acquire occult powers by the application of certain unguents to the eyes and to the feet, and by the use of the sword, the pill and the like. He may acquire then direct knowledge of objects which are subtle, very remote obstructed etc. Such knowledge, according to Praśastapāda, is actually derived through the sense organ and hence, should be regarded as perceptual. Such a person may also acquire knowledge about the fruition of past virtues and vicious deeds in the experiences of the living beings, of the heavens, the atmosphere and the earth as indicated by the movements of planets and asterisms. According to Praśastapāda, such knowledge is nothing but inferential.

In short, if the knowledge is dependent upon an invariable mark it becomes included in inference. If it is independent of any such mark, it can be included either in perception or in intuitional cognition.[12]

Praśastapāda also refers to a view according to which definite cognition (*nirnaya*) is accepted as a distinct form of valid knowledge. It is not clear which system accepts such a view. Praśastapāda however offers a definition before rejecting the above claim. It is a cognition which is produced from the perception of some specific characteristics, is definite or certain in nature and opposed to doubt. The author of *Vyomavatī* explains that an error also is definite in nature and opposed to doubt, but it is not produced from the perception of a specific characteristic. Thus the definition is not applicable to error. The commentator further points out that the definition may indeed be applicable to valid knowledge in general and in that case the expression 'opposed to doubt' becomes redundant, because the knowledge being valid is not deviating. But the defends the definition by saying that actually a distinct form of ascertainment, namely, an ascertainment which is acquired after dispelling a doubt, is meant here.[13] From his remarks it appears that this form of cognition is admitted by the Nyāya. In fact, in the list of sixteen categories in the first *sūtra* of the NS, we find one called *nirnaya*. It is defined as the determination of the right nature of an object after having an initial doubt about it through the thesis (*pakṣa*) and the antithesis (*pratipakṣa*).[14]

As Vātsyāyana comments :

"*Sādhana* means establishing one's own thesis and *upālambha* means refuting the opponent's thesis. These two, *sādhana* and *upālambha*, are referred to by the words thesis and anti-thesis in the *sūtra*, because they depend on and are related to the thesis and antithesis and are employed for ultimately establishing one of the alternatives (i.e. the thesis). Of these two, one is ultimately to be rejected and the other is to be established. Thus, the final ascertainment is the determination of the contention of that which is established".

In short, it seems that ascertainment is to be divided into two groups, one preceded by doubt and the other not so. Śrīdhara also appears to hold a similar view, though his comments are very brief.[15]

Praśastapāda argues that it is nothing distinct. In fact, definite cognition only can be of two types, perceptual inferential. If one has a perceptual knowledge of the specific characteristic and the doubt is dispelled by it, it will be a case of perceptual ascertainment. For example, in a certain object standing at a distance, one perceives only the common characteristics of a post and a human being, e.g. same height etc. and there is no awareness of the specific characteristic of any one. However, later one perceives in the object the head, hands and feet etc. which are the specific characteristics of a human being. The doubt is dispelled and the object is definitely cognised as a human being. It is a case of perceptual ascertainment. Secondly, in the forest, in an animal hidden by the bushes, one may only perceive the horns. Then, one may have a doubt about the animal, whether it is a cow or a *gavaya*. Afterwards, when one perceives only the dewlap, one ascertains, taking it as a mark, that the animal is a cow. This is an example of an inferential ascertainment. Thus, there is no scope for the contention that *nirṇaya* is a form of distinct cognition.[16]

Verbal Testimony (*Śabda*)

We have already noted that different systems accept different forms of valid knowledge or *pramāṇa*. To justify the Vaiśeṣika view that there are only two forms of valid knowledge Praśastapāda has shown that some of the other forms admitted by others can be included in any of the two, specially in the inferential.

For example, word or knowledge derived through words (*śabda*) is accepted as a distinct form by most of the systems. But actually it should be included in inference. The process for deriving knowledge through inference and also through words are the same. A person who has earlier ascertained invariable concomitance has later a definite definite knowledge of the mark and also has a recollective cognition of that concomitance can have an inferential knowledge about an object which is not perceptible. Similarly, a person who is able to derive knowledge through words must ascertain beforehand that a particular word has invariable concomitance with a particular object. He must have also a definite cognition of the word and recollect that this word is invariably related to this object. Thus, when one becomes aware of an object on hearing a word it is similar to deriving the knowledge of fire from the knowledge of smoke.[17]

Praśastapāda's description is naturally simple, but the commentators have to defend it against the contentions of the opponents. As we have already noted verbal testimony is accepted as a separate *pramāṇa* by the majority of the systems. Accordingly, all the major commentators elaborately discuss the various arguments for and against the Vaiśeṣika view.

For example, some opponents argue in the following manner.[18] It has been said that knowledge derived through words is really inferential cognition. But, as everybody will agree, in an inference, there is the cognition of the subject (*dharmin*) as qualified by the inferable property. What exactly would be the subject in the inference of an object (signified) from the word? The meaning, i.e. the objects signified, cannot be the subject of inference, because at the time the inference is being put forward the meaning is not yet known. In every inference the subject must be known beforehand; otherwise the inference itself cannot proceed. If the hill remains unknown how can one infer fire from smoke there? The meaning of the object is known only after the inference has been successfully put forward. Therefore, the meaning cannot be claimed to represent the subject.

It would neither be justified to claim that word is the subject of inference. In that case, possession of meaning or object (*arthavatta*) would have to be accepted as the inferable property. But it would not be proper to do so. No relation, such as, conjunction, inherence etc, can be established between a word and an object. Hence, one cannot establish by inference that a particular word possesses a particular object. In the inference of fire in the hill it is possible to do so, because the relation of conjunction exists between the two. In short, here it is not possible to have knowledge of a subject as qualified by the inferable property. The relation between the word and the object is actually the relation of the signified and the signifier (*pratipādya-pratipādaka-bhāva*). But this relation can be established only after the meaning has been ascertained from the word, and not before. As such the knowledge of the meaning cannot be derived through the words.[19]

Moreover, as is wellknown, fire is inferred from smoke because there is invariable concomitance between the two. But no such concomitance can be established between a word and the meaning, because there is deviation with reference to space (*deśa*) and time (*kāla*). For instance, even though there is no Yudhiṣṭhira living in the present Kali age, yet we find that the word *yudhiṣṭhira* is used in the same sense. Again, for instance, the word *cora* is used by the people of the south to mean cooked rice, but the people of eastern India use it to mean a thief.[20]

Verbal testimony cannot be included in inference also because of another fact. What does establish the validity of an inference? An inference becomes valid when a correct mark has been offered and this correctness of the mark is determined by its possession of the three essential characteristics of a valid mark (which we have already discussed). In the case of verbal testimony however validity is not proved in such a manner. A statement by itself is neither true nor false. Its validity or invalidity depends on the nature of the speaker. If he is a trustworthy person (*āpta*), has valid knowledge about the objects he is describing, and does not suffer from any defect like the desire of cheat, incapability of the senses etc., words uttered by him will produce valid knowledge. In short, the validity here is dependent upon the trustworthiness of the speaker. Thus, there is difference in the very nature of the two sources of knowledge and as such, they should be treated as two separate types.[21]

Before giving his final reply and indicating the exact form of the inference which shows that verbal testimony is not distinct from inference, Śrīdhara gives an example which is undeniably a case of inference, but objections as to the exact subject may be raised, in the same manner.

When the forefinger is raised, there is produced an (inferential) cognition of number ten with regards to things not present at that time and place. In this case also, the number is not the subject, because it is not yet known. Nor can the particular position of the forefinger be regarded as the subject, because it is something that is being known at that very moment, and not beforehand. In an inference the subject must be something already known. Besides, there is also no such relation between the forefinger and the number so that one may be inferentially known as qualified by the other. The two are accompanied by each other neither with reference to time nor with reference to place. Yet it is a fact that when the tradespeople conduct business the raising of the forefinger invariably produces the knowledge of the number ten. It cannot but be a case of inference and some sort of invariable concomitance between the two must be there.[22]

It may be argued that the above case is a genuine

inference, because it is really based upon concomitance. It is already known that whenever a person raises the forefinger, he intends to convey the number 'ten' and when an observer finds that a person has raised the forefinger he becomes aware of the intention of that person and accordingly understands the number 'ten'. To this, Śrīdhara remarks that the same is true of verbal cognition also. For example, when the word *go* is uttered, one comes to recognise the fact that the speaker wishes to indicate a certain animal with the hump etc. This recognition again is due to the fact that we have invariably found that the utterance of the word *go* is originated by an intention of conveying that animal. This intention leads to the inference of the animal. According to Śrīdhara, here the inferential argument may be formulated as follows: the subject, the person concerned, has the intention of conveying the animal with the hump etc., because he is the prosnouncer of the word *go*, just like myself.[23]

There may be an objection. In the case of unreliable persons, we find that they often have the intention of conveying things which have no real existence. Thus the mere presence of intention cannot indicate the existence of the object, there being no actual concomitance between the two.

Śrīdhara contends that the objection applies even if we consider verbal testimony as a separate source of knowledge. Words are often used by mistake. A word may be used to indicate an object with which it has really no connection. This may happen not only in the case of an ignorant person, but also in the case of the learned if he has an intention of cheating. In other words, no definite relationship between a word and an object is established. Thus, even if word is accepted to be a separate *pramāṇa*, valid knowledge may not be produces from a word.

As against the above, it may be pointed out that not any word is capable of producing valid knowledge. There is a vital condition. Only when a word is spoken by a reliable person it becomes a source of valid knowledge. A reliable person is one who is free from ignorance, the desire for cheating etc. Hence, the objection does not hold good.

In answer, Śrīdhara points out that the objection may be avoided by those who do not accept word as a separate *pramāṇa* also in the same manner. They may say that an object is rightly known from the intention of only such a person or speaker as is trustworthy or reliable.[24]

As to the objection that there is no invariable concomitance between a word and an object, because the same word may be used in different senses in different countries, Śrīdhara's answer is as follows. Smoke is indicative of fire because of a natural relationship between the two. It is true that this is not possible in the case of the word and its meaning or object. Still, a word becomes indicative, like a gesture, when it is used in accordance with a certain convention made by the intention of the persons concerned. Through the intention of the speaker, a word indicates only that thing with regard to which the said convention has been fixed. It is only when the word is used by a reliable person that it has invariable concomitance with the object, just as, it is only when the smoke is found to rise upwards in a continuous volume that it is indicative of fire.[25]

Moreover, though the object conveyed by the word *cora* may not be the same in different places, there is no difference in the process of deriving right knowledge through that word. A person from the north may understand a thief by the word and a person from the south may understand cooked rice by the word, still, both derive the knowledge of the objects inferentially.

In the *Kiraṇāvalī* Udayana also has elaborately presented and defended the Vaiśeṣika view that verbal testimony is not a separate source of knowledge. He has critically examined and tried to formulate the exact forms of inferences which show that the purpose of verbal testimony is very well served by inference. He has further discussed in details the view of the Naiyāyikas who accept verbal testimony as a distinct *pramāṇa* and examined their objection to the inferential formulations offered by the Vaiśeṣikas. Udayana's role is interesting. In the *Kiraṇāvalī* he is a follower of the Vaiśeṣika and has to defend strictly the Vaiśeṣika stand. But he has also discussed in details about the *pramāṇas* admitted by the different systems of Indian philosophy in one of his independent works, namely, the *Nyāyakusumāñjalī*. In this work, he is a staunch Naiyāyika and has to defend the Nyāya position against the views of all other systems including even the friendly Vaiśeṣika. Thus he has there to controvert the Vaiśeṣika view and find fault with the inferences offered by the Vaiśeṣika.

The peculiarity in the case of knowledge derived through verbal testimony lies in the fact that when one listens to a statement one does not just understand the individual meaning of each word, but also comprehends a mutual relation among them so that the statement presents a new or whole meaning. Those who accept verbal testimony as a separate source generally insist that this mutual relation cannot be known by an inference. Udayana examines some inferences which may be offered by the Vaiśeṣika in order to show that the mutual relation of the meaning also may be reached by an inference.[26]

For example, an inference in the following form may be offered (after listening to a statement one may infer): These meanings are mutually related, because it is a sentence (*vākyatvāt*). The idea is that the meanings as signified by the words in the sentence must be mutually related, because the words represent a sentence, and a sentence always expresses a connected or whole meaning. But Udayana points out that this inference is not technically correct. The reason here is 'because it is a sentence', but it is not present in the subject (*pakṣa*) of the inference, namely, the meanings. We have here the fallacy of *svarūpāsiddha*.

This difficulty may be avoided by changing the reason: 'because they are meanings signified by words.' Here the underlying concomitance is, whatever is a meaning signified by a word is related to another meaning. But there can be no such general rule. For example, one utters the words *gaur aśvaḥ*; a person listening to them understands the meaning of each word, but does not have any awareness of a mutually related meaning. In other words, in the present case, there would occur the fallacy of the irregular (*anaikāntika*). The same is true of another possible reason, namely, 'because they (the meanings) are recollected through words.' In the same example one recollects the meaning when one listens to the words signifying them, but there is no comprehension of a connected meaning.

A further inference may be presented from the Vaiśeṣika point of view: these words (*pada*) are characterised by the mutual relation of the meaning recollected, because they lead to the recollection of those meanings. But this inference also is unacceptable, because it is not possible to state exactly what is sought to be established by the inference (*sādhya*). The idea is that here a sort of relation among the meanings conveyed by the words is being sought to be established. But what would be this relation? None of the recognised relations, such as, conjunction, inherence, identity or the relation of qualifier – qualified, is possible here. Thus, due to the absence of any *sādhya* the inference falls through.[27]

Finally, representing the Vaiśeṣika view, Udayana says that the proper inference in this case may be stated as follows: these meanings are mutually related, because they are recollected by words which are characterised by expectancy (*akāṅkṣā*), compatibility (*yogyatā*) and proximity (*āsatti*); as in the case of the sentence *gām abhyāja*. It is generally found that when the words have expectancy etc., one understands a whole or connected meaning from such words. Therefore, whenever one listens to some particular words having these characteristics one infers that there must be relation among the meanings. In this inference the subject is represented by the meanings (*padārtha*). Udayana says that it is also possible to offer an inference with the words (*pada*) as the subject. Thus, it may be inferred, these words are such that lead to the knowledge of a mutual relation among the meanings recollected, because they are qualified by expectancy etc. and also lead to the recollection of meanings.[28]

As we have already noted, Udayana, in fact, refers to these two inferences in the *Nku* and objects to their validity from the Nyāya stand point. In the *Kiraṇāvalī* also he reproduces the same Nyāya arguments. He remarks that, as against the above inferences of the Vaiśeṣika, the Naiyāyikas raise objections.

As to the first inference[29] (these meanings are mutually related etc.), they ask, what exactly is to be established by the inference – the invariable rule that they must be related, or, the possibility that they may have a mutual relation? The first alternative is not tenable, because there is deviation in the case of words spoken by an untrustworthy person. In other words, in the case of words spoken by such a person one does not have the awareness of a mutually related meaning. Thus it cannot be claimed that whenever one recollects meanings through words one has invariably such an awareness. Of course, it may be argued that the difficulty may be avoided by adding a qualification, namely, the words must be such as are spoken by a trustworthy person. But this also does not offer a way out of the difficulty, because until there is the awareness of the whole meaning of the sentence, there can be no ascertainment of the trustworthiness of the speaker. In fact, such a defence would lead to mutual dependence. To ascertain that the speaker is a trustworthy person one must acquire first the knowledge that this person possesses the right knowledge about the meaning of the sentence. On the other hand, if there is no ascertainment of trustworthiness of the speaker, there can be no ascertainment of the meaning of the sentence. Here a trustworthy person does not simply mean one who is free from the desire of cheating; it is rather necessary to determine for certain that his knowledge is true or valid. But such knowledge is not possible for a person who is not omniscient, because all ordinary persons are subject to error.

The second alternative that the inference is intended to establish the possibility (*yogyatā*) of getting related meaning is also not justified, because even if it is concluded that such a possibility is established, it cannot be claimed that actually there is produced an awareness of a related meaning. But the fact is that when a person listens to words he definitely understands a related meaning but not simply the possibility. Thus, the purpose of verbal testimony cannot be served by this inference. Moreover, it is to be noted that such a possibility is already proved even before the inference is put forward. If it is not so, then, it would not have been included in the expression stating the reason of the inference. The reason would have been stated simply as, 'because the words have expectancy and proximity.' In that case, again, there would have been irregularity in the case of the sentence 'sprinkles with fire' (*agninā siñcati*). Here we have both proximity and expectancy, but there is no awareness of a related meaning, because there is no compatibility or the possibility of getting connected. Fire can never be the instrument in the act of sprinkling. Such a possibility must be present beforehand; otherwise the inference itself cannot proceed.

Objection may be raised against the second inference also. There, in the expression stating the reason, expectancy has been included. But what exactly is to be understood by expectancy? It cannot be identical with the qualifier – qualified relation. In fact, such a relation is the inferable property of the inference put forward. It is not yet established, it has to be established. Therefore, it cannot be included in the reason. It can neither be claimed that it means the capability of being related as the qualifier and the qualified, because it is already covered by the inclusion of compatibility in the reason. In that case, the separate mention of expectancy and compatibility would become redundant.[30]

It is also not possible to define expectancy as one being not present without the other (*avinābhāva*). From the sentence *nīlaṃ sarojam* we get a connected meaning although there is no invariability between 'blue' and 'lotus'. A lotus may be other than the blue and the blue also may be other than the lotus. Of course, it may be argued that invariability is possible because here the general (*sāmānya*) is brought in by the specific (*viśeṣa*). The term *nīla* stands for a quality in general and term *saroja* stands for a substance in general and there is invariability between a quality and a substance. But this claim also is not acceptable. In that case, there would be difficulty in certain cases-where there are really two sentences, there will be the objection of taking it to be a single sentence.

Even if we leave aside the question of an exact definition

of expectancy, there are difficulties in accepting the second inference. Thus, It may be asked, for getting a related meaning, is it sufficient that expectancy is *present*, or is it necessary that it is to be *known* as such? If the first alternative is accepted, there is no need to include it in the reason, because like the self – mind conjunction etc. it would be the cause by mere presence (*sattāmātra*).[31]

The second alternative also is not logical. This alternative would have been acceptable if it could have been shown that even though expectancy is present, there is no awareness of a related meaning due to the absence of its knowledge. For example, as it happens in the case of inference in general, it is not enough that concomitance is there, it is to be ascertained also and then only an inference becomes possible. But it is not actually so in the case of expectancy. It is observed that even when expectancy is there (but is not known), there may be an awareness of the related meaning provided that there is definite knowledge of only proximity and compatibility.[32]

So the contention of the Naiyāyika is that verbal testimony is to be accepted as a separate source of knowledge. Its purpose cannot be served by any inference.

Finally, Udayana says that the Vaiśeṣika position is that the point sought to be established by the first inference is the invariable rule that the meanings *must be* related. There will be no irregularity because the further qualification that the words are to be spoken by the trustworthy person is also to be added. In other words, when a person listens to a group of words which are characterised by expectancy etc. there is always an awareness of a related meaning provided that the words are spoken by a reliable person.

As we have already seen the Naiyāyikas have objected to the addition of this qualification. But Udayana contends that even the Naiyāyikas have to accept the fact that the words, if they are at all capable of conveying a related meaning, have to be spoken by a reliable person, and this is to be admitted even if verbal testimony is accepted as a separate source of knowledge.[33]

Thus, a question may be put to the Naiyāyikas, namely, when it is said that meanings are understood from words, is it intended that meanings are understood simply from words, or from a special kind of words, i.e. words which are spoken by reliable person. The first alternative cannot be accepted, because in the case of words spoken by an unreliable person there is no awareness of meanings. There is a definite awareness of a related meaning only when the words come from a reliable person. Thus the reliability of the speaker has to be taken into account somehow.

Of course, the Naiyāyikas may try to avoid the difficulty by pointing out that even though the words may be spoken by an unreliable person there is indeed an awareness of the meaning. This is because one is found to engage in activity even from the statement of such a person. If there is no awareness of meaning at all, how would an action be possible on its basis? The question of the reliability of the speaker comes in later. One may have a doubt regarding the validity of the meaning understood and one may not be able to get into action with certainty. In such a case to ascertain the validity or invalidity of the statement one may be led to enquire whether the words have been spoken by a reliable or an unreliable person. In short, so far as the understanding of the related meaning is concerned, the specific nature of the speaker need not be taken into account.[34]

From the Vaiśeṣika standpoint Udayana contends against the above that such a position would lead to absurdities. For example, in the case of inference also it may be argued that the mark itself, without any ascertainment of concomitance, leads to the knowledge of the inferable property. So far as the production of inferential knowledge is concerned there is no necessity of ascertaining the concomitance. Later, if there is a doubt regarding the validity of the knowledge acquired, then only the question of there being concomitance or not has to be considered. This is to be admitted also because it is actually observed that a person may engage himself in a particular action even though the knowledge may be produced by a pseudo-mark and not a valid mark.

But, obviously, such a position is not acceptable even to the Naiyayikas. They also have to admit that smoke as such cannot be a valid mark for the knowledge of fire; it can be so only when it is established that there is invariable concomitance between the two. Thus the right conclusion would be that a mark as is free from any condition (*upādhi*) and is characterised by invariable concomitance can really lead to the knowledge of the inferable property. The same analogy has to be accepted for the case of verbal testimony also. It is not that any word simply is capable of conveying the intended meaning, for in that case even the word 'jar' may express the meaning 'a piece of cloth'. Nor can it be said that whatever leads to the awareness of a meaning is a proper word, because, in that case, it would not be possible to make any distinction between a good word (*śabda*) and a bad word (*apaśabda*). Therefore, the logical position would be to maintain that a particular word produces the awareness of a particular meaning only when the convention (*saṅketa*) that this particular word expresses this particular meaning has been laid down by the trustworthy person. Thus if a meaning is to be understood from words the nature of the speaker has to be taken into consideration, and in that case the purpose of verbal testimony may well be served by inference.[35]

The author of the *Vyomavatī* holds a unique view in this regard. He says that it cannot be definitely said that Praśastapāda includes verbal testimony in inference. For this, he offers a rather clever explanation of the expressions used by Praśastapāda. Praśastapāda says that *śabdādi* is to be included under inference. In this expression we have a Bahuvrihi compound, which again may be of two types *tad–guṇa–saṃvijñāna* and *atad-guṇa-saṃvijñāna*. If the first type is accepted then only it can be said that Praśastapāda speaks of inclusion into inference of not only some other *pramāṇas* but also of verbal testimony as well. However, if we accept the second type, then the implication would be that all other so called forms of *pramāṇa* excepting verbal testimony are to be included into inference. The commentator, as it appears from the long discussion that follows, is definitely inclined to accept the view that verbal testimony is a separate source of knowledge, even though he dose not deny that there is a great similarity between the inferential process and the process of acquiring the knowledge of meaning through words.[36]

Finally, he distinguishes between verbal testimony and inference in the following way. When one acquires knowledge through some statement and may have a doubt whether it is true or false, what one does to remove the doubt is to enquire about the nature of the speaker. If one finds that the speaker is reliable one concludes that it is true. On the other hand, if one ascertains that is spoken by an unreliable person one concludes that it is false. But in the case of inference the process is different. If one has a doubt regarding the validity or invalidity of an inferential knowledge, One enquires about the nature of the mark employed–whether it has concomitance, whether it is present in the subject, and so on and so forth. Therefore the sources of these two cognitions should represent different *pramāṇas*.[37]

Validity of Veda

As it is wellknown both the Vaiśeṣika and the Nyāya systems are included in the Āstika group of Indian philosophy, which means that they accept the authority and validity of the Veda. Perhaps that is why, although according to these systems the Veda also comes under verbal testimony, both add some special comments establishing the validity of the Veda. In the *Nyāyasūtra* one section is devoted to establish the validity of verbal testimony in general,[38] and again, in addition to it, there is a separate section to prove that the special form of verbal testimony, i.e. Vedic statements also are valid.[39] Praśastapāda deals with the problems very briefly. Even then, after stating the conclusion that verbal testimony is nothing other than inference, he makes some brief comments regarding the validity of *śruti* and *smṛti*.

Praśastapāda says that the above forms of scriptural statements also are dependent for their validity upon the trustworthiness of the speaker. As Śrīdhara brings out the implications, it is not that ordinary statements only convey their meanings on the strength of the trustworthiness of the speaker, but even the scriptural statements of the above forms convey their meanings on the strength of the same quality. Words as such are neither good nor bad; such characters are not inherent in them like the bad smell of some foul thing. A statement becomes true or false according as the speaker is reliable or unreliable. If the speaker is reliable his statement also would be correct and lead to valid knowledge. If the speaker is unreliable his statement would be false and it will not lead to valid knowledge. In this regard, ordinary statements and scriptural statements have the same status.[40]

It may be objected that Vedic statements are of a special kind. The Veda is eternal and it has actually no speaker.

Therefore, the question of its invalidity does not arise at all. Its validity is thus intrinsically established. If it were the work of some author, we could never ascertain it to be of absolutely undoubted authority, for it is generally found that people often make false statements under the influence of attachment and aversion.

With this objection in mind Praśastapāda quotes *sūtras* of Kaṇāda which substantiates his view.[41] According to Śrīdhara, the implication is that the scriptural statements are spoken by seers (*ṛṣi*) who are a special kind of speaker, quite different from ordinary speakers like ourselves. Clarifying further the commentators says that validity is due to absence of defects, and not to eternality. For example, the auditory sense and the mind are both eternal, but they may become defective due to some adventitious circumstances. Again, the visual sense may be non-eternal, but when the defect has been removed from it. It becomes a valid means. It can be shown that there may be some superior persons who are free from all defects. Since the scriptures are spoken by such persons they must be valid in spite of having connection with some person. It can never be doubted that a person who sees the reality of things and has conquered attachment and aversion, when moved by compassion to guide the people of the world, could impart wrong or false teachings.[42]

How is it known that the scriptures are composed by some superior persons? It is inferred from the fact that the implications of such statements are universally accepted to be true, without any dispute, by men belonging to every caste and stage of life. If it were composed by an ordinary person it would not have commanded such respect and one would not have been engaged to action, without hesitation, on its basis. When all men are agreed on the point of its authority or validity, a statement cannot but be accepted as the source of valid knowledge.[43]

It is wellknown that the Mīmāṃsakas reject the view that Veda is the composition of any being. Its validity therefore cannot be due to its being the words of a reliable person. In fact, its validity is intrinsic. It is argued that when some action prescribed by Veda is performed, even the most learned people have no idea of any author. In the case of some ancient texts like the *Rāmāyaṇa* or the *Mahābhārata* the author may not be actually perceived by anybody, still authors are remembered through the ages up to the present time. But in the case of *Veda* even such remembrance is not possible. Therefore, *Veda* must be without any author.

Śrīdhara does not mention the name of the Mīmāṃsaka, but records the objection.[44] He argues that with the intention of refuting the objection Praśastapāda quotes another *sūtra*[45] of Kaṇāda which clearly shows that like ordinary compositions Veda also has an author and it is also not eternal as claimed by the Mīmāṃsaka. That it is non-eternal is proved by inference, Like ordinary compositions Veda also is a collection of sentences. All sentences are found to be composed by intelligent persons, who compose them according to their intellect and intentions. No sentence is ever found to be without any author. Veda also should not be any exception. Praśastapāda also quotes another *sūtra*, which states that certain words are found to be employed in Veda and they are always spoken by some intelligent person. In ordinary use also they are found to be employed by such persons. In Veda also they should be so.

The author of *Vyomavatī*, though defending the validity of Veda on the ground that it is the composition of a reliable person, thinks that the implication of Kaṇāda's *sūtra* quoted in this context is different.[47] He contends that Kaṇāda actually points to God as the author of *Veda*. Ordinary statements are not always valid; they may be true or they may be false. This means that ordinary persons are liable to error. They may be misguided by attachment or aversion. But Vedic statements are always valid and never false. Therefore, they must have a speaker who is *infallible*, never influenced by any defect. Such a person can be none other than God. Moreover, a speaker to be reliable must have a direct experience of the things he speaks about. But in the Vedic statements many extraordinary things are spoken of and it is not possible for ordinary persons to have any direct experience of them. In other words, the author of Vedic statements must be an omniscient being. This also indicates that the author of Veda must be none other than God.

Udayana also argues in the same manner. According to him also, the infallibility of Veda cannot be defended unless God is admitted to be the author. As it is wellknown, not only in the *Kiraṇāvalī* [48] but also in the Nku which is specially designed to establish the existence of God, one of the principal argument offered for God is the authorship of Veda. In this work Udayana has discussed the matter with much elaboration.[49]

Thus it appears that we have two lines of interpretation, one offered by Śrīdhara and the other by the *Vyomavatī* and Udayana. The first makes the Vaiśeṣika an atheist, but the second makes it theist. In this context, it is to be noted that there is no conclusive proof to establish that the Vaiśeṣika system admits the existence of God. No early commentary on the VS is available and the later commentators are naturally influenced by much later traditions and try to show that Kaṇāda also accepts God. But so far as Praśastapāda is concerned he does not seem to recognise God at least as the author of Veda.[50] He clearly states that Veda is the composition of seers who are of course not ordinary persons like ourselves. Not only in the present context, but also later while explaining the nature of *ārṣajñāna* Praśastapāda categorically mentions the fact. There is no scope for doubt, because the plural number is used, indicating that Veda is not the composition of a single person like God but is the production of so many authors. Śrīdhara's explanation therefore seems to be more logical and less far-fetched.

Others forms of valid knowledge

Praśastapāda very briefly refers to certain other sources of knowledge which are recognised by some as distinct ones, but he includes them in inference. For example, gesture (*ceṣṭā*) may be a source of valid knowledge.[51] When somebody places his folded palms near the mouth one looking at him arrives at the knowledge that the person is thirsty. This knowledge is not perceptual; it is not inferential, for no such process involving an invariable mark is present and finally, as there is no statement it cannot be a case of verbal testimony also. Therefore, it should be an independent source of knowledge.

But Praśastapāda rejects the claim and says that it is really a case of inference. The particular movement of the body or its limbs is invariably related to certain facts. When a particular gesture is made it is taken as the ground of inference and the fact invariably related to it becomes the inferable property. Apparently, there is found no inferential process, but this is due to the fact that an experienced person can go through the process of inferring so quickly that he seems to acquire the knowledge without any such process. But that is really not the case. The process is there but because of constant practice it is performed without the least delay.

Comparison (*upamāna*) is one of the *pramāṇas* which is admitted by the majority of Indian systems of philosophy.

However, the Vaiśeṣikas include it in inference. Praśastapāda's remark regarding comparison is very brief; in fact, confined to a single sentence.[52] He says that a reliable person speaks of a *gavaya* to a person who does not know the animal through a cow and hence it is nothing but the statement of a reliable person. The remark is rather cryptic. The commentators have explained it invariably in the light of the various later conceptions of comparison. When it is said that a *gavaya* is described through a cow the possible implication is that the similarity between the two animals is pointed out. The knowledge of similarity leads to the identification of the *gavaya* in the case of a person who does not know the animal. But it is clear that knowledge is ultimately derived through the statement of a person who actually knows the animal and hence, is reliable. Of course, Praśastapāda does not categorically say that it is inference (*anumāna*), but is identical with verbal testimony (*āptavacana*). But as we have already seen that verbal testimony is not a distinct form and is covered by inference, we have to conclude that comparison also is a kind of inference.

One of the systems recognising comparison as a distinct *pramāṇa* is the closely allied Nyāya system. According to it, the distinct function of comparison is to generate the knowledge of the relation between the naming word (*saṃjñā*) and the object denoted by it (*saṃjñin*).[53] Briefly, the process is as follows. A person knows the cow well but does not know the *gavaya* i.e. does not know which animal is denoted by the word *gavaya*. A forester who knows the *gavaya* well tells him that the *gavaya* is similar to the cow. This statement is called *atideśa-vākya*. Later, the person who has heard the statement goes to the forest and comes across a *gavaya*, and perceives its similarity with the cow. This leads to the recollection of what he had earlier heard from the forester. He then knows that the animal before him is called the *gavaya*, i.e. he ascertains that the particular animal in front of him is denoted by the word *gavaya*. Nyāya argues that this ascertainment of the relation between a word and an object cannot be the result of either verbal testimony or inference. It is produced by a separate form of *pramāṇa*.

Śrīdhara refers to this contention of Nyāya, but naturally does not accept it. He argues that the knowledge is really derived through inference aided by verbal testimony. The statement that the *gavaya* is similar to the cow, which is held to give rise to the cognition 'that which is heard as *gavaya* is similar to the cow', this cognition can not but be regarded as purely verbal in character. As for the cognition of the denotability of the animal similar to the cow by the word *gavaya*, it is purely inferential. The inferential form is as follow: A word becomes expressive (*vācaka*) of that with reference to which it is used without any opposition by all the learned persons; the word *gavaya* is so used with reference to an animal similar to the cow. Therefore, the animal must be denoted by the word *gavaya*.[54]

Śrīdhara continues and says that the cognition of similarity in the *gavaya* is undoubtedly perceptual in character. As for the cognition of the relation between the name and the named, it is a case of recollection produced by the impression generated by the cognition of denotability by the word *gavaya* of the animal similar to the cow, brought up by the previously born commonality, manifested by the comprehension of similarity. In all this there would be no room for comparison and as such, it cannot be accepted as a separate *pramāṇa*.

The author of *Vyomavatī* also refers to the Nyāya view and rejects it. While describing the Nyāya view, he points to the objection that if comparison is not accepted as a separate form and it is argued that the knowledge of denotability is derived from the statement of the reliable person itself, then, there will be a contradiction with one of Kaṇāda's *sūtras* which states that perception of the object is a necessary condition for its getting a name.[55] At the moment the statement is made by the forester the *gavaya* is not perceived. Still, he argues that the knowledge of denotability is produced by the statement itself. The statement conveying similarity really means that whatever object is similar to a cow is to be expressed by the word *gavaya*. Since he acquires thus the knowledge of denotability he makes the usage 'this is a *gavaya*' when he finds an animal as characterised by similarity with a cow. The question of contradiction with Kaṇāda's *sūtra* does not arise, because there perception does not mean perception alone, but stands for any reliable instrument of knowledge. In fact, a name can be applied even if the object is not perceived, e.g. a father gives a name to his son though he may be far away at the time the son is born.[56]

As we have already seen, in the case of verbal testimony Udayana plays a double role, as a Vaiśeṣika and as a Naiyāyika. The same is true in the case of comparison also. In the *Kiraṇāvalī* he defends the Vaiśeṣika view against the view of the Naiyāyika, but in the NKu he does the opposite. In the former, he quotes arguments from the NKu establishing that comparison is a separate source of knowledge and rejects them one by one.[57]

Those who argue that comparison is a separate form emphasise the point that the knowledge of the relation of denotability in the wellknown example cannot be derived through any other means. Two factors are involved here; first, the statement of the forester which is of the nature of verbal testimony and secondly, the perception by the villager in the forest. It cannot be said that the relation of denotability is known simply from the statement, because in that case even one who has never seen a *gavaya* should derive knowledge regarding denotability. It cannot also be argued that the knowledge of denotability is derived simply from the perception of the animal, because in that case it would have to be admitted that even a person who has never listened to the statement of the forester should acquire knowledge of denotability. If can neither be argued that the knowledge is derived through a combination of the two, because as they occur in different times a combination is obviously impossible.[58]

It may be argued that though the statement is not present later when the perception occurs there may be a recollection of the meaning of the statement at that time and with its assistance the perception of similarity would produce the knowledge about the relation of denotability and there is no need to consider comparison as separate. As against this, the Naiyāyikas point out that if in this case the knowledge is accepted to be derived from verbal testimony or perception, then, the same can be maintained in the case of inference etc. also. An inferential process also involves perception (i.e. perception of the mark) and recollection (i.e. recollection of invariable concomitance). Should we then not consider inference also as a separate source?[59]

Moreover, the statement of the forester conveys similarity only, but this similarity cannot be considered the criterion for applying the term *gavaya* (*pravṛtti nimitta*). The actual criterion for applying the term is *gavayatva* which can not be known either through verbal testimony or perception. Comparison alone can make it known. Similarity cannot be such a criterion because in that case a person who has never seen a cow and does not know about the similarity would never be able to use the term *gavaya*. It cannot also be argued that both similarity and gavayatva are to be considered as the criterion; in the case of the forester it is the later, but in the case of the villager it is the former. In that case the forester's statement conveying similarity would be unjustified, because from the usage of the learned he has ascertained only the *gavayatva* is the criterion. He has not learned that similarity is so and hence while communicating what he has learned he should not make a statement involving similarity.[60]

In short, the function of comparison cannot be accomplished by any other source of knowledge.

However, from the Vaiśeṣika standpoint, Udayana argues that the knowledge of denotability is really derived from nothing but the statement. From the statement itself the forester ascertains that the term *gavaya* is a name for that which is similar to a cow, and later in the forest when he comes across the *gavaya* he only has its recollective cognition.

The final option of Udayana seems to be that when a person listens to the statement that a *gavaya* is similar to a cow one has a doubt whether the similarity is only an accidental qualification (*upalakṣaṇa*) or a criterion for applicability (*nimitta*). But it has been already shown that the similarity cannot be such a criterion. Hence, the person concerned fails to construe the meaning of the sentence in its primary sense and takes the help of secondary meaning. In other words, he determines that in a secondary sense similarity with a cow actually stands for *gavayatva* which is the criterion. As such, there is no need to accept comparison as a separate source.[61]

Praśastapāda next takes up the case of postulation (*arthāpatti*), which is accepted as a separate *pramāṇa* by the Mīmāṃsakas. Here also the statement is very brief, limited to only a few words.[62] However, the two major types of *arthāpatti* are most probably referred to. In later tradition postulation is generally divided into two types *dṛṣṭārthāpatti* and *śrutārthāpatti*.[63] When a fact which is established by any *pramāṇa* other than verbal testimony, but can be justified only by postulating some other fact it will be of the first type. Since the Mīmāṃsakas admits six kinds of *pramāṇas* the first type would be of five varieties, the initial fact being established by any of the *pramāṇas* other than verbal testimony. When the initial fact is known through verbal testimony and some other fact is postulated to justify it, we shall have an example of the second type.

Śrīdhara refers to a wellknown example of the first type. It is learned that a person called Caitra who is alive is not present in the house. The absence of Caitra in the house is known by the *pramāṇa* called negation (*abhāva*). The knowledge as regards his being alive indicates the possibility of his presence in the house because a living person is generally found to be present in a house. But it is not possible for the same person to be both absent and present in the house at the same time. Thus the absence would be inconsistent with the information regarding the man being alive if he did not exist somewhere outside the house. Thus Caitra's absence from the house is justified only on the assumption of his presence outside the house. This ascertainment of presence cannot be due to any accepted form of *pramāṇa*. It is acquired by postulation.[64]

According to Praśastapāda, the above would be a case of inference based on the contradictory (*virodhin*). Caitra is definitely known to be alive and as such, he must be present somewhere, he cannot be totally absent. Absence from the house and presence outside are mutually contradicted. When one is denied the other is established. There is a universal rule in this regard. When Caitra's absence from the house is affirmed his presence outside is confirmed by the rule of contrary. It is thus a case of inference.

The wellknown example of the second type of postulation is as follows. A person listens to the statement that the fat boy called Devadatta does not eat during the day. The fatness is inconsistent to with the fact of not taking any food. It is therefore justified by postulating the fact that Devadutta eats during the night. The ascertainment regarding the taking of food in the night cannot be known through any other *pramāṇa*. This type also is rejected as a separate source. It is included in an inference based upon inference (*anumitānumāna*). The idea seems to be that fatness is first inferred on the basis of the statement, and on the basis of fatness in its turn the fact of eating at night is inferred.[65]

According to Śrīdhara, the implication is that the inconsistency of a *pramāṇa* lies in its incapability to bring about the cognition of its objects. The statement 'Devadatta does not eat during the day' is found to be quite capable of conveying what it is meant to convey. As such, there is no possibility of inconsistency which the Mīmāṃsakas may accept as the ground for the assumptive cognition of eating at night. In other words, there is at all no scope for postulating another fact.

It may be objected that there is inconsistency. Fatness, the effect of eating, would not be possible without eating in the day because there is no other cause for fatness. This impossibility would make the statement in question also inconsistent as it is not in keeping with the real state of things.

In reply, it is pointed out that if we accept the above it would have to be admitted further that inconsistency of a statement lies in the improbability of the meaning, and its consistency in the probability of its meaning. There would be no consistency or inconsistency in the statement itself. Thus the meaning or the object in the form of fatness of one who does not eat in the day, being an effect of eating, becomes consistent or probable by reason of the meaning or object in the form of eating at night, and not by reason of the statement that Devadutta eats at night. As a result, what the inconsistency or improbability of the object would need for the justification of itself and its expressive statement would be an object and not a statement, a statement cannot justify the inconsistency of an object. In the case in question, the object in the form of fatness of one who does not eat in the day is found to be invariably an effect of eating at night. There is no scope for admitting postulation based on verbal testimony as it can be explained by inference.[66]

Another *pramāṇa* which seems to be accepted by some, but not at all by any of the wellknown systems, is concurrence (*sambhava*). According to some, it is proposed by the Paurāṇikas and is supposed to explain an ascertainment in the form since there are one thousand people in this crowd there are one hundred. A thousand is never possible without a hundred. According to Praśastapāda this is clearly a case of inference, because it is based on invariable concomitance.[67]

According to some, a separate form of *pramāṇa* called negation (*abhāva*) has to be admitted. Praśastapāda simply says that it is a form of inference and makes no further comment as to its nature or illustration. However, in Vātsyāyana's commentary we find an example. According to him, when something is known as the contrary of something else it would be a case of negation. For example, the knowledge of non-occurrence of rain leads to the knowledge of conjunction between the wind and cloud, because there is no falling of rain-water in spite of its heaviness when such a conjunction exists as the obstructing factor. Generally, because of its heaviness, rain–water falls to the ground. However, it does not rain when there is a strong wind which forces the cloud to move away. Thus, from the knowledge of the non-occurrence of the rain is ascertained the presence of conjunction between a strong wind and cloud. Praśastapāda explains its inclusion in inference by saying that the appearance of the effect leads to the inference of the presence of the causes and in the same way, the non–production of the effect leads to the inference of the absence of the causes. There is invariable concomitance between the presence of the causes and the appearance of the effect. Similarly, there is also invariable concomitance between the non–production of effect and the absence of causes.[68]

Another source of knowledge which is generally referred to and refuted in almost every text of Indian philosophy, but is never found to be positively defended by any system, is traditional saying (*aitihya*).[69] It is generally illustrated by a statement preceded by the expression 'thus it is said', such as, 'a spirit dwells in this tree'. It no doubt resembles verbal testimony very much but the idea seems to be that since no speaker of the statement is traceable it cannot be included in verbal–testimony. So it should be taken as a separate source. In refutation, it is pointed out that even though this speaker may not be actually available, it cannot be accepted that it is without a speaker. The main point is whether the information given by the statement is true or false. If the statement is false it would follow that it is not the statement of a reliable person and naturally it cannot at all claim to be considered a *pramāṇa*. On the other hand, if it is true it would follow that it comes from a reliable person, though his identity may not be known and as such it should come under verbal testimony because it conforms to the definition. However, the Vaiśeṣikas consider verbal testimony as included under inference and hence traditional saying would be a kind of inference for them. According to Nyāya it would naturally be verbal testimony.[70]

NOTES & REFERENCES

1. *Vyomavatī*, p. 212.
2. Ibid, p. 213.
3. NK, p. 626.
4. NS, 3.2.41, gives a long list of factors which give rise to recollective cognition. According to Śrīdhara, they also are to be taken into account here.
5. NK, pp. 625-26.
6. PPbh, p. 626 and NK thereon.
7. See the next chapter, last section.
8. PPbh, p. 628.
9. NK, p. 629.
10. *Vyomavatī*, p. 214.
11. Ibid.
12. PPbh, p. 630
13. *Vyomavatī*, p. 211.
14. NS, 1.1.41.
15. NK, pp. 623 f.
16. PPbh, pp. 622 f.
17. Ibid, p. 512 and NK thereon.
18. NK, pp. 513 f.
19. Ibid.
20. Ibid.
21. Ibid.
22. Ibid.
23. Ibid, p. 515.
24. Ibid, p. 516.
25. Ibid.
26. *Kiraṇāvalī*, p. 572.
27. Ibid.
28. Ibid, p. 573.
29. NKu, 3.13 and Udayana's own explanation; *Kiraṇāvalī* p. 573.
30. NKu, 3.13.

31. Udayana on ibid.

32. Ibid.

33. *Kiraṇāvalī*, p. 575.

34. Ibid and under NKu, 3.13.

35. *Kiraṇāvalī*, p. 576.

36. *Vyomavatī*, pp. 163, 164.

37. Ibid, pp. 165, 171.

38. NS, 2.1.49 – 56.

39. Ibid, 2.1.57 – 68.

40. NK, p. 519. See also NS 2.1.68 and Bhāṣya thereon.

41. VS, 1.1.3 Commentators like Śaṅkara Miśra and others explain the *sūtra* in a totally different way and accept it as a definite proof for the existence of the God as admitted by Kaṇāda. However, so far as Śrīdhara is concerned there is no ambiguity that he considers *Veda* to be the composition of the seers.

42. NK, p. 520.

43. Ibid.

44. Ibid, p. 521.

45. Obviously, the reference is to VS 6.1.1. However, the reading of Praśastapāda does not agree with that of the printed editions.

46. VS, 6.1.3.

47. *Vyomavatī*, p. 168.

48. *Kiraṇāvalī*, p. 578.

49. NKu, almost the whole of the second *stavaka*. In this connection almost all the commentators criticise the theory of intrinsic (*svataḥ*) validity of *pramāṇa*.

50. In the case of Kaṇāda it is doubtful whether he actually admits God or not. But Praśastapāda definitely admits God, though in a different context. There can be no creation without the will of Mahesvara. See PPbh, *Sṛṣṭisaṃhāra-prakaraṇa*.

51. PPbh, p. 529 and NK thereon.

52. Ibid, p. 530.

53. See, for example, NKu, 3.10. Bhāṭṭas also admit *upamāna* but for a different reason. According to them, similarity (*sādṛśya*) is a distinct category and it can be known only through *upamāna*. The view is refuted by Udayana in NKu.

54. NK, p. 533.

55. VS, 2.1.19. The reading of the *sūtra* in the printed editions is however different.

56. *Vyomavatī*, p. 177.

57. *Kiraṇāvalī*, pp. 588 ff. See also NKu, 3.10 – 12.

58. Ibid.

59. Ibid.

60. Ibid.

61. *Kiraṇāvalī*, p. 589.

62. PPbh, p. 534.

63. See, for example, MM, NK and *Vyomavatī*.

64. NK, p.535.

65. Ibid, p. 537.

66. Ibid, pp. 538 ff.

67. PPbh, p. 542.

68. Ibid.

69. Ibid, p. 558.

70. For a similar discussion on the exact number of *pramāṇas*, see also, NS, 2.1.1-12.

CHAPTER FIVE

Invalid Knowledge And Its Forms

We have already seen that, according to Praśastapāda, knowledge is mainly divided into two classes, valid (*vidyā*) and invalid (*avidyā*). Each of them again is divided into four forms. The four forms of invalid knowledge are: doubt (*saṃśaya*), error (*viparyaya*), indefinite knowledge (*anadhyavasāya*) and dream (*svapna*).[1]

On Doubt

Before we discuss the view of Praśastapāda on the nature of doubt and its varieties, it would not be irrelevant to see in brief what Kaṇāda says about this form of invalid knowledge. Of course, Kaṇāda does not give any classification of knowledge and he points to the special characteristics of doubt only incidentally, most probably indicating the fact that a critical examination is generally preceded by a doubt.

In the *sūtra* generally describing doubt, he indicates the conditions that give rise to doubt, which are apprehension of common characteristic, non-apprehension of specific characteristic and recollective cognition of specific characteristic.[2] For example, in an object standing erect in the distant field a person may perceive height etc. which are common to both a tree and a human being, he does not perceive the specific characteristic of either, such as, branches, leaves etc. or hand and feet etc., although he recollects the specific characteristics of each. In this situation he will experience a doubt: is the object a tree or a human being.

According to the commentators, in some of the following *sūtras* Kaṇāda has also given a classification of doubt. Different commentators give different illustrations and it is not easy to form an idea about Kaṇāda's views.[3] First, doubt is divided into two classes, external and internal. The first again is of two types, relating to something either perceived or not perceived. For example, someone listens to the statement 'a man has come' and then, he has a doubt (when I go out) 'shall I find this person to be known or unknown to me?' Again, someone finds that a man has come, and looking at him, he has a doubt 'am I looking at a person already known or unknown?' Sometimes a doubt may be based on past and present experiences. For example, a man called Devadutta has been first seen with hair, afterwards with the head shaved and again later with hair. Next, on hearing that Devadutta has come, one may have a doubt whether one will find him with hair or with a shaved head.

Śaṅkara Miśra comments that in the case of an external doubt the object may be either perceived or not perceived. An example of the first would be the doubt whether the object standing in the field is a tree or a human being, after one has ascertained the common characteristic of the two. But when one looks at only the horns of an animal, but the animal is hidden by the bushes one has a doubt whether the animal is a cow or a buffalo. It has also been pointed out that sometimes the common characteristics the apprehension of which gives rise to doubt belongs to more than one object, e.g. the doubt whether it is a tree or a human being. But when there is a doubt if Devadatta will be found with hair or without hair, the common characteristic, namely, being Devadatta, belongs to a single object.

However, it appears that the commentators who are much later are influenced by Praśastapāda's explanation. Whatever might have been the actual implication of Kaṇāda they have tried to explain his views in conformity with that of later authors.

In the list of sixteen basic categories given by Gautama doubt occupies an important position. Its importance is pointed out again and again by Gautama and his commentators. Gautama speaks of five types of doubt and the classification is based on a different principle.[4] There also the commentators are not unanimous in interpreting the *sūtra* of Gautama. The Vaiśeṣika commentators have tried to show that Kaṇāda's position is free from objections and though there may be some difference of opinion with the Nyāya there is indeed no serious difficulty.

Coming to Praśastapāda we find that according to him also the conditions giving rise to doubt are almost the same. He also admits that in the case of doubt there should be previous knowledge of the specific characteristics of two things, only the common characteristic of the two should be known to be present in a certain object and there should be a recollective cognition of those specific characteristics. The last implies that there should be no ascertainment of the specific characteristics, for it would actually dispel the doubt. However, he adds one more condition, namely that a doubt is the result of *adharma*.[5] Commentators explain that the purpose of this addition is as follows. Doubt is a form of invalid knowledge and its acquisition is not something desirable or conducive to pleasure. It is rather a source of suffering. Hence, it must be produced by *adharma*.

Śrīdhara has explained the position of Praśastapāda very well.[6] Praśastapāda says that doubt results from the perception of *mere* similarity. The addition of the word *mere* implies that there should not be any apprehension of this specific characteristic. The word 'perception' also is not to be taken in the sense of direct knowledge or sense-perception, but in the sense of apprehension in general, for even if the common characteristic is known by an inference or any other means of knowledge there may be a doubt. The cognition of similarity implies the cognition of an object in which the similarity is present, because in the absence of the cognition of the object, there can be no cognition of the similarity by itself. The doubt also pertains to the object and not to *mere* similarity, because it is distinctly and definitely recognised, and with regard to it there can be no doubt.

The word 'similarity' indicates only the possession of a common characteristic, which is however not something inhering in many objects, because with regard to a single object, namely, the self, one may have a doubt as to whether it is without touch and minute or large (*mahat*), the doubt being due to the fact that absence of touch is found both in *ākāśa* which all-pervasive or large and the internal organ (*manas*) which is minute.

The upshot of all this is that when a person perceives in an object a certain property which is common to it with another object, and by some reason or other fails to perceive the specific characteristics of that object and then, remembers the two objects as perceived on some earlier occasion as possessed of contradictory properties. He ascertains that there is no possibility of these properties being present in a single object because they are contradictory. Nor does he ascertain the non-existence of them because he actually perceives the common properties concomitant with them. At that moment having definitely cognised the object as possessing the common properties there arises in his mind an uncertain feeling as to that object being possessed or not of its specific characteristics. This uncertain feeling is called doubt.

Praśastapāda divides doubt in two classes, namely, external and internal.[7] According to Śrīdhara, the five kinds of doubt admitted in the Nyāya system are covered by them. He also explains the example of internal doubt given by Praśastapāda. An astrologer, after finding some speciality in the position and motion of the planets and stars, is found to make certain predictions as to a certain event having happened, happening or likely to happen (i.e. in the past, present and future) and he finds that they turn out to be true. On another occasion however he finds that his deduction from the same causes turn out to be false. Then, when on a third occasion he makes similar predictions from the same causes, he himself has a doubt regarding his own knowledge based on those marks whether it is true or false.[8]

External doubt is of two kinds, pertaining to a perceptible object and pertaining to an imperceptible object. Praśastapāda explains it as follows: in the case of an imperceptible object, a doubt arises from the perception of some common mark the recollective cognition of the specific characteristics of both and *adharma*. For example, when in the forest, a person sees the horns only he has a doubt whether the animal is a cow or a *gavaya*. In this case, the object is hidden from view by something like a large tree or bushes etc. and its character is only inferred from the sight of the horn. Hence, the object of doubt is said to be imperceptible. In a certain object presented before the eyes, a person perceives only the common characteristic of a post and a human being, namely, the same height; does not apprehend any specific characteristic, such as, crookedness etc.; there is thus no manifestation of the universals like post-ness etc., but, due to the recollective cognition of the specific characteristic of the two, he is equally drawn to two alternatives and his awareness swings from the one to the other - is the object in front of me *post* or a *human being*?[9]

The author of *Vyomavatī* analyses the nature of doubt further. A question is raised: is doubt a single piece of knowledge, or, a collection of more than one cognition? It may be argued that the latter alternative should be accepted because two pieces of cognition are found to be produced gradually, 'it is a post' and 'it is a human being'. But in that case there will be a problem. One of the alternatives revealing the object as it really is will represent a valid cognition and being the opposite of the other would negate it. As a result, the doubt itself would be destroyed. The commentator therefore says that, though involving alternatives, a doubt actually represents a single piece of knowledge. The recollective impression brings about the recollection of two opposite special characteristics and there is produced a single cognition referring to the two.[10]

As we have already remarked, the treatment of doubt in Nyāya is different. In the first chapter Gautama gives one *sūtra* referring to the different types of doubt as produced from different causes. We shall note them here very briefly for a comparison.[11]

The first form of doubt is due to the apprehension of common characteristics. Somebody perceives, in an object, the common characteristics of a post and a person, namely, a certain height and breadth. He becomes desirous of ascertaining the distinguishing characteristic of each as previously perceived. He fails to affirm definitely either of the alternatives and has a cognition in the form: is it a post or a person? Such an indecisive (*anavadhāraṇa*) cognition is doubt. According to Vātsyāyana, a special form of knowledge is conducive to such doubt, namely, 'I apprehend the common characteristics of two objects, but do not apprehend the distinguishing characteristic of each.' It is easy to see that this form of doubt is the same as one given by Praśastapāda. In fact, in the majority of cases, a doubt generally assumes this form.

The second form of doubt is due to the apprehension of a unique characteristic. Vātsyāyana illustrates it as follows :

"The unique characteristic of earth is smell, which distinguishes it, on the one hand, from water etc. (similar objects), and on the other, from quality and action (dissimilar objects). The unique characteristic of sound (*śabda*) is being caused by disjunction (*vibhāgajatva*). One doubts whether sound is a substance or a quality or an action because the unique characteristic is found to act both ways (i.e. as distinguishing the object from both the similar and the dissimilar). (One wavers among the alternatives:) is sound, being a substance, distinguished from quality and action? Or, is sound, being a quality (distinguished from substance and action)? Or, is sound, being an action (distinguished from substance and quality)?"

The person concerned only perceives the characteristic of being produced by disjunction, which is a unique characteristic of sound. But he does not perceive in sound the special characteristic of either a substance or a quality or an action. Hence, there arises a doubt regarding the nature of sound.

This form of doubt has not been admitted by Praśastapāda. However, commentators point out that, though Gautama recognises a form of doubt in the above manner, it is not necessary for Praśastapāda to admit it, because as we shall presently see he has accepted a different form of invalid knowledge called *anadhyavasāya*, and the second form of doubt actually represents such a knowledge.

The third form of doubt is said to be due to contradictory statements about the same object (*vipratipatti*). For example, someone says that the self exists. Again, someone says the self does not exist. A person listens to both the statements but cannot find any ground proving either of the alternatives. But the presence of both existence and non-existence in the same locus is impossible. In such a circumstance, the failure to ascertain the truth takes the form of doubt: Is the self existing or non-existing?

Next, doubt may also be due to irregularity of apprehension (*upalabdhi-avyavasthā*). For example, one apprehends water in the tank etc. where it actually exists. One also apprehends water in a mirage where it does not actually exist. Therefore, after apprehending an object somewhere and not finding any proof determining the existence or the non-existence of the object, one doubts whether the object apprehended is existent or non-existent.

Similarly, doubt may be also due to irregularity of non-apprehension. For example, things like the root of a tree, water etc. though existing under the ground are not perceived. Again, an object which is yet to come into being or which has been destroyed is not perceived. Therefore, after non-apprehending an object somewhere and finding no decisive proof one doubts whether the object which is not apprehended is actually existent or non-existent.

Uddyotakara has not accepted the above interpretation of Vātsyāyana. According to him, Gautama admits only three types of doubt, i.e. those due to apprehension of common characteristics, due to apprehension of a unique characteristic and contradictory statements. Irregularities of apprehension and non-apprehension are really a general condition for all the three forms. Irregularity of apprehension and irregularity of non-apprehension respectively mean the absence of any definite proof establishing an alternative and the absence of any definite proof rejecting an alternative.

After elaborately discussing the nature of doubt according to Gautama, Uddyotakara further quotes Kaṇāda's *sūtra* giving the general definition of doubt and remarks that there is no opposition with the definition offered by Gautama and hence, Gautama's definition also covers the one given by Kaṇāda. He also argues that if Kaṇada's *sūtra* is rightly interpreted it will be found that he also admits the second form of doubt, i.e. doubt due to the apprehension of a unique characteristic.[12]

However, it is not easy to accept the opinion of Uddyotakara. So far as Kaṇāda's definition is concerned it is clear that he admits only a single form of doubt. Śaṅkara Miśra has shown how all the forms of doubt may be reduced to a single one. He has also criticised Uddyotakara by name. Secondly, it is also clear that according to Gautama doubt is of five types. In the second chapter, in the critical examination of doubt, Gautama takes up each of the five one by one, mentions the objections against each and finally provides answers to them.

On Error

We have already noted that, according to the Vaiśeṣika, the *pramāṇas* are only two, perception and inference. Praśastapāda does not explicitly give any general definition of error, but comments that error also may be related to cases of perception and inference. He brings out the nature of error in the two cases by explaining some examples. For example, when somebody ascertains a cow as a horse it will be a case of perceptual error. Of course, in the long statement enumerating the causes of such a wrong ascertainment Praśastapāda seems to give a general definition of error, which is: an awareness of something in an object which it is really not.[13] Various factors are responsible here. First of all, one must be already aware of the specific characteristics of the two objects, e.g. one must already know that the special feature of a cow is the dewlap and that of the horse is the mane. In spite of having the knowledge of these specific characteristics one fails to identify the object rightly, because one's senseorgans are deranged by such causes as bile, phlegm and wind. Being a form of knowledge there should be present also, as the general cause, a contact between the self and the mind, which again must be assisted by the impression produced by the knowledge of the object which is not present before the observer. Since error is not a desirable object, *adhrama* is also included in the list of its causes.[14]

Śrīdhara has explained the process in the following manner. The sense organ, the visual in the present case, comes in contact with a cow, but does not perceive the universal of cowness in it, perceives it only as a body as qualified by similarity with the cow. Due to this cognition of similarity the impression as regards the horse is awakened. When the recollective knowledge of the horse has been produced, the said impression brings about the cognition of the horse by reason of the similarity of the horse in the cow, which is in direct contact with the sense organ. This is really due to some mental defect. Thus it is that everything is not (wrongly) cognised everywhere, the necessary restriction being done by similarity and previous impression.[15]

It also explains why such an error is called sense-born. It could not be sense-born if it were to take cognisance of the universal of horse-ness only without being related to any substratum, i.e. a horse (which is not present before the eyes of the observer); or, if it belonged to a person the activity of whose sense organs have all ceased. As a matter of fact, we find that it takes cognisance of the horse in the body of the cow which is in contact with the fully active visual organ. It is thus undeniable that the error is sense-born.

It should be noted also that Śrīdhara refers to his view of error as *viparītakhyāti* and distinguishes its from *asatkhyāti*.[16] He contends that in error always one thing appear as what it is not. Even in a case where an error arises without any sort of objective substratum it is something *not existing* which is cognised in the contrary form, i.e. as *existing*. This cannot be a case of *asatkhyāti* or a cognition of the non-existing, because the object as such is always likely to exist, and it is never possible for the non-existing to be cognised.

In a case where we have an error appearing in a certain objective substratum, we have similarity as its cause. But in a case where there is no objective substratum and the error is due solely to mental derangement, there is no possibility of any cognition of similarity, e.g., when a man infatuated with love for a woman perceives his beloved here, there and everywhere. An impression is the cause only in cases where the error is determinate. But when it is indeterminate the cause is only the derangement of the sense organ, because an error is always found to be accompanied by some such defect e.g. when a person has the notion of yellowness in the conchshell.[17]

The above is an example of (we may say) a normal error. But Praśastapāda gives another example of error which is of a special kind in the sense that here there is no actual perception, still one has the wrong awareness of perceiving something, e.g. when one perceives the sky as a mass of darkness.[18] This example is also explained by commentators. For example, Śrīdhara says:

"A man due to a desire of observing the sky directs his

eyes upwards, and the visual rays having gone to a great distance become slackened in their speed; and then, being struck by the powerful light-rays from the sun shooting in an opposite direction (downwards), they are turned back. They render perceptible the blue quality of the ocular orbs which is without any substratum; and then, it is that they produce the cognition that the sky is free from clouds and appears like the calm ocean, a cognition in which we have what appears like a perception of colour in the sky which is really imperceptible.

"That the sense-organ of vision makes the quality of its own orb appear as inhering in the sky is proved by the peculiar character of the cognition which is found to follow the qualities of the sense-organ. For instance, a man with jaundiced yellow eyes sees the sky as besmeared with molten gold; and a man under the influence of cold and phlegm having his eyes whitened perceives it to be like silver. Then, again, when a man looks upon the deep darkness of night, he perceives what he thinks to be a mass of collyrium, though in reality there is absolutely nothing there.

"And this is a case of perceiving as perceptible what is imperceptible."[19]

In this connection the author of the *Vyomavatī* examines and refutes a view which appears to be very similar to *akhyātivāda*. It may be argued that an error is impossible, because there can be no cause productive of an error. The senseorgans are by nature capable of producing right knowledge only, i.e. the knowledge of something in a thing which it really is and they are incapable of producing an error. It cannot be argued that they produce a cognition which is opposite in nature (i.e. invalid), when they are deranged by defects like jaundice etc., because when a cause is defective it is not productive of an effect at all. For example, the seeds of *śāli* if they are soaked in oil fail to produce the sprouts of *śāli*, but are never found to produce the sprouts of *yava*. Similarly, if the senseorgans are not defective, they will produce right knowledge, but if they are defective they would not produce something of a different kind. Moreover, there is no ground to suppose that the (wrong) cognition of the silver has as its underlying object (*ālambana*) the shell. Therefore, what happens really is that a kind of recollective knowledge, namely, this is silver, is produced. Here 'this' represents the knowledge of similarity and 'silver' represents a recollective cognition.[20]

Refuting the above view the commentator says that it is unacceptable, because in that case this specific activity of a person desirous of collecting silver cannot be explained. When a person has an erroneous cognition of silver in the shell he goes on to collect the silver without hesitation and this proves that he definitely identifies the shell as the silver. It cannot be said that he simply fails to distinguish between the two pieces of cognition (perceptual knowledge of similarity and recollective knowledge of silver) or cannot perceive the distinction between the objects of cognition (the shell and the silver), because an absence of knowledge cannot lead a person to any activity; a person is led to an activity by a definite form of knowledge.[21]

The objection that the knowledge 'this is silver' cannot have shell as its underlying objects is also not well founded. Afterwards, when the wrong cognition is removed, the person may have a recognition in the form 'this shell appeared to me as silver'. Moreover, since the knowledge in the form 'this is not silver' can have the shell as its object, the knowledge in the form 'this is silver' also has to be accepted as having the shell as its object. If it were not so, the negation in the form 'this is not silver' would not have been possible, because there would have been no possibility (*prasakti*) of its presence. Unless there is a possibility of presence there cannot be a negation.[22]

The objection that there is no cause capable of producing an error also does not make sense. The cause-effect relation between two things is ascertained through agreements in presence and in absence. Through such agreements it is determined that it is the sense-organs that produce right cognition when they are not defective, and in the same way it is determined that when the sense-organs are defective they produce wrong cognitions. It is ascertained by direct observation that the same sense organs produce different kinds of effects under different circumstances. Therefore, it cannot be said that error is an impossibility.[23]

Next, Praśastapāda gives two illustrations of error as relating to an object of inference. Thus, vapour may be mistaken for smoke and from it the presence of fire may be inferred, and also the sight of the horns of a *gavaya* may lead to the inference that the animal is a cow. In such cases what is not an actual mark is taken as the actual mark as a result of which the inference becomes wrong.[24]

Finally, Praśastapāda has given some more examples of error which are, in fact, more interesting. He says that error may be produced also due to the study of false philosophical doctrines. Thus, he says:

"With regard to the tenets of the Buddha and others which are opposed to those of the Vedas, some people have the idea that they are conducive to actual welfare, and this also is an instance of wrong idea, an error. So also are the following: the notion of self with regard to the body, the sense organs and the mind; the idea of eternality with regard to caused things; the idea of the appearance of effects in the absence of adequate causes; the idea of evil with regard to persons advising what is really good and the idea of good with regard to those who counsel evil ways."[25]

Commentators have explained the implication of the above with interesting examples. For example, in the systems of Śākya, Bhikṣu, Nirgranthaka, Saṃsāra-mocaka and the like, which are all opposed to Vedic tradition we find teachings which they propagate as truly good and desirable. But if anybody accepts them to be really so, it would be a case of error according to the Vaiśeṣika. The ground for their rejection is that they are accepted by very few people, they are deprecated by others and they speak against *varṇas* and *āśramas*, and finally they are contrary to all proper reasoning.

Similarly, the view that the Veda is eternal as advocated by the Mīmāṃsaka is an error, because the Veda is really non-eternal. The Cārvākas do not admit *adṛṣṭa* as a cause and it is also a case of error because in that case an effect would be produced without a cause. Some sects advise the bearing of dirt, mud etc. and some advise committing suicide. But all this amounts to error, because such advice is really harmful for one.

On Indefinite Knowledge

In the case of indefinite knowledge also we do not have much besides examples. As in the case of error, here also Praśastapāda says that such knowledge occurs with regard to objects perceptible and inferable.[26]

In the case of the perceptible, again, the object of such Knowledge may be either already known or not already known. Such knowledge is of the form 'what is it' and is of the nature of a mere acquaintance (*ālocanamātra*). It occurs when the observer's mind is specially attached to something else or he is desirous of acquiring some further specific information.[27]

Alter giving this general idea about the nature of indefinite knowledge Praśastapāda gives an example of such knowledge only in the case of an object not already known. An example with regard to an object already known is given by the commentators. The king is wellknown to a person. The king passes by along with his retinue, but the person, being preoccupied with some other matter, fails to recognise him, though he is aware that some important person has passed by, and subsequently has just an awareness 'who is it that has just passed by.[28]

Praśastapāda has given the illustration of an indefinite cognition as regards an object which is not wellknown rather explicitly. According to him, in the case of such an object the indefinite knowledge appears on account of ignorance. For example, an inhabitant of the Vāhīka country has no definite idea of the jackfruit tree, even when he is standing in front of one and has many definite cognitions with regard to its various aspects, such as, it exists, it is a substance, it is a modification of earth, it is a tree, it has a certain colour, and it has branches etc. Even the generic character of jackfruit *panasatva* is perceived as present in all jackfruit trees and also as absent from all other kinds of trees (though indeterminately). It is only the fact of its bearing the name of jackfruit that he does not know, because no one has instructed him to that effect, though he has only the idea that the thing in front of him must have a name. This knowledge devoid of the idea of the particular name is what is known as indefinite cognition.[29]

An example of indefinite knowledge with regard to an inferable object is given similarly. For example, there is no cow in a place called the Coconut Island. An inhabitant of the island comes to a different country where cows are available. He does not perceive the cow but only has a sight of the dewlap. He infers that it must be a kind of animal and he has also the knowledge of the general properties as belonging to animals, but due to lack of instruction, fails to ascertain that its name is 'cow'. He has only an indefinite knowledge, namely, what exactly may be this animal.[30]

Thus, it appears that finally an indefinite knowledge is the absence of the definite knowledge of the name of the object. Commentators have not also offered much information on this kind of knowledge; specially, no commentator has tried to explain why it is to be accepted as a distinct form of invalid knowledge. However, all the commentators have tried to show, through very briefly, that such knowledge is to be distinguished from doubt.[31] It is distinct from doubt because of two reasons. First, it is produced from different causes. A doubt is produced from the knowledge of similarity etc., but in the case of such knowledge those factors are not necessary. Secondly, there is difference in nature also. In a doubt there must be two opposing alternatives, but in such knowledge there is no such alternatives.

According to Śrīdhara also, it would not be right to regard it as a form of doubt in spite of the fact that it is not a form of knowledge which is definite. The origin as well as the form of such knowledge differs entirely from that of doubt. A doubt arises from the recollective cognition of the peculiar characters of two objects, but there is none such in the case of such knowledge, which often arises from mere absence of a distinct cognition of peculiarities. Secondly, a doubt wavers between two alternatives, touching sometimes the one and sometimes the other, but this is not the case with indefinite knowledge.

Commentators also point out why such knowledge cannot be regarded as a kind of *vidyā*. A valid knowledge is generally the cause for a particular kind of activity; with regard to a desirable object one tries to acquire it, with regard to an undesirable object one tries to avoid it and with regard to an object which is of the nature of neither one remains indifferent. But an indefinite knowledge does not give rise to any such activity. Therefore it cannot be included in *vidyā*.[32]

We have already noted the remark of Śaṅkara Miśra that Gautama's second form of doubt is not accepted by the Vaiśeṣika, because the latter admits a distinct form of knowledge, namely, indefinite knowledge. It appears that there is also the view that such knowledge is nothing but doubt. Bhāsarvajña, for example, specifically mentions the name of *anadhyavasāya* and strongly argues that it is to be definitely included in doubt.[33]

We may have a very brief idea of the controversy:

"Kaṇāda gives an analysis of doubting judgements as arising from the concurrence of three conditions: (1) perception of something as being of a general kind; (2) failure to perceive its differentiating characteristics; (3) recollection of those differentiating characteristics.

"Praśastapāda interprets this to mean that we are in doubt when (1) we perceive that *x* and *y* have a common set of general characteristics, (2) we remember that *x* has different specific properties than *y* does, but (3) we cannot see clearly enough (or infer cogently enough) to tell whether the object of our awareness is *x* or *y*, this obscurity stemming from *adharma*.

"He distinguishes doubting judgements from indefinite ones – the latter, he says, occur when we do not know the word for a thing and thus describe it in vague terms. Vyomaśiva expands on this last point – doubt is always about objects of a kind we are already acquainted with, while indefinite judgements may also be about objects of a kind we never before confronted.

"Later writers relax the distinction between doubting and indefinite judgements, however. Vallabha has it that the only difference is that indefinite judgements have the form of a question – is this a dagger I see before me? – while doubting judgements have the form of a disjunction – this is either a dagger or a mirage. And Śivāditya merely includes indefinite judgements as a subclass within doubting ones."[34]

On Dream

The last and fourth type of *avidyā* is dream – cognition. Praśastapāda has discussed it in some details. He has described the situation in which such a cognition originates and has also given a classification depending on the special cause which may give rise to it. He has also given a number of interesting examples.[35]

First he briefly mentions what is exactly meant by a dream–cognition. He says that when a person's senseorgans have ceased to function in respect of their specific objects, and the mind has retired, then there arises a certain mental cognition through the instrumentality of the senseorgans themselves, and this is what constitutes a dream-cognition.

Explaining the process further, Praśastapāda says that beings tired by their exertions during the day as caused by their conscious bodily actions, retire at night with a view to either resting or enabling their food to the digested, and then the connection of the self with the internal organ, brought about by an effort due to the force of the unseen (*adṛṣṭa*), causes certain functioning in the mind; and then the mind remains without any action in a certain portion of the self, namely, the interior part of the heart which is without any connection with any of the external senseorgans. The mind having thus retired (*pralīna*), the senseorgans of the person concerned cease to function. In this state, the processes of inbreathings and outbreathings go on continuously from such causes as sleep (*svāpa*) which is the name of a particular state of a contact of the self with the mind and impressions of previous cognition; as a result, there appears, through the sense organs, a dream-cognition, which is of the nature of direct sense-cognition, with regard to objects which have no real existence (*asat*).[36]

As regards objects which have no real existence, the author of Vyomavatī notes some different interpretations. According to some, such objects simply mean which though cognised to be present there are not actually so, e.g. an elephant etc. Others think that in a dream-cognition an object is revealed in the form of something else which it is really not, e.g. when the wall is presented as an elephant. An object which has no real existence means here that an object is not possible in that particular form in which it is being presented.[37]

However, the author of Vyomavatī is not in favour of this interpretation. He argues that there is no ground to suppose that the wall etc. are the actual objects of a dream-cognition, but they are presented in the form of the elephant etc. A person walking up after a dream does never remember his experience in the form that the wall etc. appeared to me in the form of the elephant etc. In that state the external senseorgans cannot naturally function and produce the knowledge of the elephant etc. in the wall etc. A dream cognition takes place only when such sense organs have ceased to function. The internal sense also cannot be responsible for such knowledge, because it cannot independently function in respect of external objects.[38]

The same commentator also refers to an objection to

admitting dream-cognition as a form of *avidyā* distinct from error etc. If it is admitted to be simply a knowledge of something which it is really not, then it should be called an error. If it takes the form of a cognition referring to two opposite alternatives it will obviously be included in doubt. Again, if it assumes the form 'I do not exactly know or cannot name what it is' it is to be considered as indefinite cognition. In short, a dream-cognition does not represent an additional form. Why then has it been mentioned separately? The answer is that some dreams indicate auspicious things and some inauspicious, and therefore, it is mentioned separately.[39]

This view also does not find favour with the commentator. He argues that a dream-cognition is produced from some distinct causes of its own and hence it is to be accepted as a separate form. If the cause is different the nature of the effect also must be different. An error is produced concerning perceptible and inferable objects in respect of a person whose senseorgans are incapacitated due to some defect. A doubt also is produced concerning the same objects when there is the apprehension of common characteristics, but no apprehension of a specific characteristics. An indefinite cognition also has specific causes of its own. As has been explained above, a dream-cognition also is produced from a specific set of causes and hence, it is to be accepted as sharing a different nature.[40]

According to Praśastapāda, dream-cognitions are of three kind as they depend on three different causes.[41]

The first one is said to be due the strength of impressions left by previous cognition (*saṃskāra-pāṭava*). It is illustrated when some person who is, for example, in love with a woman, or when he is very angry with his enemy, thinks constantly of his beloved or his enemy, and while thus thinking goes to sleep, then the series of thoughts or mental images appear, by the strength of the impressions left on his mind, in the form of the direct sense-cognition of something directly in contact with his organs of perception.

The second type is said to be due to the disorder of bodily humours. The humours of the body are serum, flesh, fat, marrow, bone and semen. These are also called *dhātu* because they hold or support the body *(dhāraṇāt)*. When they are deranged by the disorders of wind (*vāta*), bile (*pitta*) and phlegm (*kaha*), there appear certain mis-conceptions. Thus, a man in whose constitution wind is the predominating factor or one in whom the element of wind is subject to disorder by some cause or other perceives as if he were floating in the sky or running about here and there. Again one who is of a bilious temperament or one in whom the element of bile has been developed abnormally perceives as if one were entering into fire and sees such things as mountains and orbs of gold, the solar disc and so forth. One of a phlegmatic temperament or with his element of phlegm disordered feels as if one were crossing rivers and oceans and sees mountains of snow etc.

Lastly, there are dream-cognitions which are due to *adṛṣṭa*. Very often there appear in dreams certain cognitions of objects previously perceived and also of those never perceived before, of those known as well as of those that are not known. Among them, there are some, for example, the riding on an elephant, the obtaining of an umbrella and such other things, which indicate that something auspicious is going to occur very soon, and the dream-cognitions of such things are produced by previous impressions and *dharma*.

Again, there are certain things which are of an opposite nature, i.e. which indicate that something inauspicious is going to happen in near future, for example, the rubbing of oil and the riding of asses and camels etc. The dream-cognitions of such objects are produced by previous impressions and *adharma*.

However, dream-cognitions may also pertain to things absolutely unknown, which are never experienced by the person concerned or anybody else, events which can never take place in real life, e.g. the swallowing of the sun and the moon etc. Such dream-cognitions are produced by adrsta alone, there being no possibility of previous impressions.

Justifying why dream-cognitions are mentioned separately, Śrīdhara comments that though all such cognitions produced either from the strength of impressions or from the disorder of humours or from *adṛṣṭa* consists of the false imposition of an external form on that which is wholly internal, and as such, being the cognition of something as what it is not may only be considered to be a special kind of error, yet it is classed separately because it occurs only during a particular condition of the body.[42]

Another kind of cognition which also occurs under very similar circumstances and has in fact close resemblance with dream-cognition is found mentioned in the Vaiśeṣika works, called *svapnāntika*, But Praśastapāda comments that it is not to be identified with dream-cognition. As Śrīdhara explains, it may sometimes happen that a man recollects in dream what he has been dreaming of in the form 'I have been dreaming of such an such a thing'. This, being the end of the preceding dream, is called dream-end cognition. As it also appears when the senseorgans are not functioning people may be inclined to take it as dream-cognition. But it would not be proper. Being only the recalling of what has been previously cognised it should be considered as a kind of recollection (*smṛti*). [43]

In this connection we may briefly note some points about dream-cognition as noted by the followers of Nyāya. The idealists who deny the reality of external objects rely much on the instance of dream. It is argued that the cognition of an object does not necessarily prove its reality. In the state of dream one apprehends so many things as real, but on waking finds that they are not there. Similarly, to one who is under the influence of ignorance the world appears to be real, but as soon as one acquires right knowledge one finds it unreal and is liberated.

But as a staunch realist the Nyāya cannot subscribe to such a position and strongly refutes the view that dream-cognitions prove the unreality of objects. It is never denied that dreams are false experiences, but that does not lead to the conclusion that the objects experienced in a dream are absolute non-entities. Thus, for example, rejecting the instance of dream as proving the unreality of external objects, Gautama says that the awareness of an object in a dream is similar to the awareness of an object in the cases of memory-knowledge (*smṛti*) and longing for obtaining an object enjoyed previously (*saṅkalpa*).[44]

On the above, Vātsyāyana comments as follows:

"That is, (as in the case of memory-knowledge or longing, a dream-experience also) pertains to a real object perceived previously. Just as memory-knowledge and longing pertain to objects perceived previously and are incapable of disproving the reality of their objects, so also the awareness of an object in a dream pertains to a real object perceived previously and is not capable of disproving the reality of an object. And thus, dream-experiences relate to objects which are perceived to be real in the waking state. The same person who experiences dream, while asleep, also recollects, while awakened, the dream-experiences, in the form 'I dreamt of this object'.

"The awareness of the object in the state of dream is however ascertained to be false because of the appearance of a subsequent cognition in the waking state (indicating that the object of dream had not been really present there). That is, after the recollection (of the awareness in a dream) one who is awakened acquires a further definite cognition (indicating that the object of dream has not been really there); because of this further cognition there follows an ascertainment, namely, the awareness of the object in the state of dream is false."[45]

In short, objects apprehended in a dream must be objects that had been previously perceived and hence, they are not unreal.

An objection may be raised here. There is no denying the fact that one may sometimes dream of objects which one had never apprehended previously. The scriptures often give descriptions of dreams, auspicious or ominous, the objects of which had never been known beforehand. In fact, one may experience in a dream events which cannot take place in real life and of which one can have no previous experience, as for example, one may dream of cutting down one's own head or swallowing the sun.

Viśvanātha notes the objection and answers that in such cases the objects must have been known separately on some previous occasion. One may not have the prior experience of cutting down the head but one must have known beforehand separately one's own head and the act of cutting. A dream is nothing but a form of illusory perception and, in the above instance, the error lies in wrongly relating the act of cutting, actually perceived in relation to a piece of wood etc, to one's own head.

It is also clear that, according to Gautama, a dream-experience is to be distinguished from memory-knowledge. It is a form of extraordinary perception invariably produced from impression. But, as we have already seen, Praśastapāda, though agreeing that a dream is a form extraordinary perception, differs from Gautama in maintaining that all such experiences are not preceded by impressions. This is because it is possible to dream of objects which may not be experienced in real life. Such dreams are produced only from specific forms of adṛṣṭa.

In agreement with the Nyāya, Kumārila also admits that a dream invariably refers to an object previously apprehended. He even argues that even if an object of dream may not be perceived in this birth it is to be admitted as perceived in some earlier birth. An object of dream must be previously perceived in some birth, at some point of time or space. But in agreement with Śaṅkara and in disagreement with the Naiyāyika, Kumārila contends that a dream-experience is identical with memory–knowledge.

As against such identification the Naiyāyika points out that, the after-knowledge (*anuvyavasāya*) of a dream experienced by one assumes the form 'I *saw* this object', and not 'I *recollected* this object', and this indicates that a dream is a kind of perception.[46]

Nature of Recollective Cognition

We have already briefly noted that, according to Praśastapāda, recollection (*smṛti*) is clearly a form of valid knowledge. Obviously, such a position leads to various difficulties. For example, an instrument of valid knowledge is to be regarded as a *pramāṇa*. The instrument of recollective cognition also should have to be regarded as a *pramāṇa*. The Vaiśesikas admit only two *pramāṇas*, namely, perception and inference. The instrument of recollection cannot be included in either. It cannot also be regarded as a third form of *pramāṇa*, because it would go against their own accepted position.

None of the Vaiśeṣika commentators has raised or discussed such problems. Their position is rather simple: they contend that recollection is not a kind of valid cognition and hence there is no problem. In fact, the majority of the systems of Indian philosophy, with rare exception, consider recollection as a form of invalid knowledge. There is also no attempt on the part of the Vaiśeṣika commentators to explain why Praśastapāda includes recollection in the group of valid knowledge.

Śrīdhara briefly remarks that the object of recollection is invariably something which has been cognised earlier. That is why it cannot be accepted as a *pramāṇa*. It reveals an object already known and is essentially dependent upon a previous experience (*anubhava*). So far as the act of revealing an object is concerned it has nothing to reveal itself: it can reveal only the revealed.[47]

It may be objected that if dependence upon a previous experience is considered a ground for invalidity, then, inference also cannot be accepted as a *pramāṇa*, for it is also similarly dependent. Śrīdhara notes the objection and answers that an inference is dependent upon another experience for its production (*utpatti*), but so far as the act of revealing is concerned it is independent. It reveals the object on its own strength and the object revealed by it is not the same as revealed the previous experience.[48]

According to some, the, ground for considering recollection as invalid is that it is not produced from the object (*anarthaja*), i.e. the object recollected is not present at the time the knowledge is produced. Śrīdhara rejects the argument, because in that case even correct inferences referring to future and past objects would become invalid, because the objects cannot be present as in the case of recollection.[49]

The author of *Vyomavatī* adds that recollection cannot

be admitted as produced from the object (*arthaja*) because of another reason. It is obvious that recollection cannot be produced by any of the external senseorgans; it is produced through the instrumentality of the internal sense only. But the internal sense cannot act in respect of an external object without the meditation of an external sense organ. Therefore, it is better to admit that an external object has no part in producing a recollective cognition. Finally, the commentator remarks that if such a cognition were produced from an object also were non-deviating it would have been a kind of valid knowledge as produced by a *pramāṇa*.[50]

Although very little discussion is made by the Vaiśeṣikas in the present context, it is clear that the different schools of Indian philosophy are quiet concerned with the problem and they offer their own arguments for excluding recollection from the category of valid knowledge. We shall now try to have a brief idea of the different views.

According to Bhāṭṭa Mīmāṃsā, for example, this is easily done by adding the qualifying term *anadhigata* to the definition of *pramā*, which would mean that by definition a valid knowledge must be a primary and original one.[51] Recollection is not a new experience; it is only a sort of reiteration of some old experience. It has no new contents but refers to only the acquired contents of knowledge. From Vācaspati's comment in the *Tattvakaumudī* it appears that a similar position is held by the Sāṃkhya also.[52] Later followers of Vedānta also appear to adopt a similar line of argument.

The question is also much debated in the works of the Nyāya system. As the Naiyāyikas do not consider novelty (*anadhigatatva*) to be an essential characteristic of valid knowledge they have naturally to offer some different arguments. There is moreover some controversy among the

Naiyāyikas themselves regarding the actual status of recollection. Generally it is not considerd *pramā*, but there are a few who consider it to be so. For example, Viśvanātha admits that recolletion, if not contradicted, may be viewed as a form of *pramā*. If, however, recollection is vitiated by contradiction it is to be included in the category of *apramā*.

Of course, there may be an objection. If recollection is accepted to be *pramā*, its instrument (*karaṇa*) is to be recognised as *pramāṇa*. Since it cannot be of the nature of the four *pramāṇas* already recognised it would have to be taken as a distinct type. However, according to Nyāya, the instruments of valid knowledge are only four and the admission of a fifth one would go against the accepted conclusion (*siddhānta*) of the system.

Viśvanātha gives a typical answer. He says that, basically, cognitions are of two types, namely, experience (*anubhūti*) and recollection (*smṛti*). By definition, a *pramāṇa* stands for the instrument of only an experience or presentative cognition. Thus, the instrument of recollection is automatically excluded from the category of *pramāṇa*. Udayana has already given almost a similar argument. According to him, *pramā* itself is to be defined as valid presentative knowledge. Recollection, even if it is valid, is not *pramā*, because it is not presentative. Therefore, the question of considering the instrument of recollection a *pramāṇa* does not arise.[53]

Vacāspati raises the question while explaining Uddyotakara's definition of *pramāṇa*, namely, it is the cause of awareness.[54] Since recollection is a form of awareness its cause also would be a *pramāṇa*. It may be objected that a *pramāṇa* must have also an object (*artha*) as its co-operating cause (*sahakārin*).[55] But recollection is produced by impression (*saṃskāra*) and there is no co-operating cause in the form of an object. But this objection is not proper. In that case, *amumāna* and *śabda* also would lose their claim for being considered as *pramāṇa*, because both may refer to objects which are past and future. In such cases the object cannot be present as the co-operating cause.

It may be claimed that in the case of such inference or verbal testimony there may not be any direct connection with the object, still, some kind of indirect relation with it may be conceived of. For example, the relation between the inferential knowledge and the past rain may be said to be jñāpya-jñāpaka-bhāva. But this defence also is not proper. Some sort of indirect relation with the object may be conceived even for impression and recollection and accordingly, the problem remains as before.[56]

In answer, Vācaspati also claims that recollection is not *pramā* and hence, its cause is not *pramāṇa*. The relation between a particular meaning and a particular word is determined by general usage. To ascertain that a particular term is to be employed to convey a particular meaning our guide is the use of words as made by the common people. The term *pramā* is employed to mean that kind of awareness which is non-deviating from an object and is moreover specifically distinct from knowledge originating from impression exclusively, i.e. recollection.[57]

It appears that Vācaspati is not seriously involved, because the meaning of a term is not always determined by common usage; for example, in the case of technical terms employed by the different systems, the meaning of a term is fixed according to different principles.

Udayana has gone deeper into the problem.[58] He has discussed the question and some other allied problems in details, and then, given his own arguments. Thus, he asks, to the class of which *pramāṇa* should the instrument of recollection belong? The instrument of recollection is impression. It is not perception, because it does not produce a direct presentative cognition. It cannot also be identified with the three other recognised *pramāṇas*. In all these cases, the instruments, namely, the mark (*liṅga*), the similarity (*sādṛśya*) and the words (*śabda*) respectively act as instruments only after being known (*jñāta*), and not by their mere presence (*sattā*). But an impression gives rise to recollections simply by its presence. In other words, even though memory may be a form of valid knowledge, its instrument can in no way be accepted as a *pramāṇa*.

Finally, Udayana contends that recollection is not a kind of valid knowledge, because the object at the time of its apprehension and the object at the time of its recollection are not the same.[59] An object is apprehended earlier and it is recollected later. In the former it is *present*, but in the latter it is *past*. Unless the state of the object changes it cannot be designated as *past* or *present*. If it is past, it cannot be present. If it is present, it cannot be past. Therefore, although the first apprehension of the object is valid knowledge, its recollection cannot be so. Because it fails to reveal the object as previously cognised.

An opponent may argue that it is true that the previous state of the object is not there at the present moment. When the recollection occurs, the previous state of the object is not present, still recollection is valid, because it reveals the object as one the previous state of which has ceased. In short, recollection reveals an object as it actually is and therefore, it should be valid.

In answer to this, it is pointed out that recollection cannot reveal the object as one the previous state of which has ceased, because recollection can reveal only what has been earlier cognised. It cannot point to some new content, not previously known. It has not been ascertained earlier that the previous state of the object has ceased. When the basic presentative knowledge is produced, the object is naturally revealed as having its previous state intact.[60]

It has also been argued that recollection, when produced from valid experience, should be considered valid. Recollection and the experience producing it are both related to the same object (*samāna-viṣayaka*). If both the forms of knowledge have the same content, then, how is it that one is accepted to be valid and the other not? The answer to this is as follows. The object as revealed by the experience is then actually so. It is really characterised by the properties as are revealed by the experience at the time it occurs. But the recollection reveals the object afterwards, and at that time, the object has changed and the properties which were present in it are no longer there. However, the recollection fails to reveal these changes and reveals the object only as experienced earlier, i.e. being characterised by the same properties. Therefore, the recollection does not reveal the object correctly and hence, it is invalid.[61]

This is more or less the generally accepted Nyāya position. Even Gaṅgeśa has followed a similar line of argument.[62] But Jayanta Bhaṭṭa has offered his own peculiar argument, though it has not found acceptance among others.

According to Jayanta, recollection is not valid, because it is not produced due to the object it reveals (*anarthaja*). The object revealed by recollection is not present when it is produced. The object cannot be a cause for its production.[63] But in the case of perception, for instance, the object revealed is present there, the sense comes in contact with it and the knowledge is produced. It is produced by the object it reveals (*arthajanya*) and hence, it is valid.

An objection may easily be raised. Inference which is accepted as a form of valid knowledge does not necessarily reveal an object which is present there, because it may refer to objects past or future. In such cases, the inference should be considered to be invalid, just like recollection.

Jayanta himself notes the objection and answers that in the case of inference the object known is actually a thing as characterised by a property (*dharmin*). For example, when one infers past rain what one actually infers is the river as characterised by swelling, abundance of water, swift current etc. The actual object of inference, the river, is present at the time the inference is produced. Thus it is different from recollection and is valid.[64]

Jayanta himself notes another objection. How is one to explain the case of intuitional knowledge (*prātibha-jñāna*) which cannot be produced from the object of knowledge itself? For example, some one has such a knowledge in the form 'my brother will come tomorrow'. Here the object of knowledge is the act of coming, but it is yet to take place.

Jayanta answers the objection by pointing out that the difficulty can be removed in a similar manner. Here the object of knowledge is actually the brother as qualified by the act of coming. The act of coming is a future event, but the brother is a lasting object present in the three times, past, present and future. This knowledge is produced by the object in the sense that it reveals the brother who is present all along.[65]

The case of recollection is quite opposite. It can relate to an object which has long ceased to exit. The presence or absence of the object has nothing to do with the appearance of recollection. It is produced irrespective of whether its object exists or does not exist elsewhere.

Of course, Jayanta's position is not free from criticism, specially because an inferential cognition or a cognition derived through verbal testimony - when it relates to a past object - can hardly be considered to be due to the object of knowledge.

Besides, it cannot also satisfactorily explain the case of the extraordinary

perception of a *yogin*, One of the three forms of extraordinary perceptions (*alaukika-pratyakṣa*) recognised by Nyāya and it can reveal objects past, present and future. Thus such a form of perception cannot always be strictly due to the object it reveals. In fact, Jayanta himself has strongly argued in defence of the perception of a yogin.[66]

NOTES & REFERENCES

1. PPbh, p. 411.
2. VS, 2. 2.17 ff.
3. See *Upaskāra* and Candrānanda's *Vṛtti*.
4. NS, 1.1.23.
5. PPbh, pp. 411ff.
6. NK, p. 419.
7. PPbh, p. 412.
8. NK, p. 421.
9. PPbh, p.413.
10. *Vyomavatī*, p. 120.
11. NS, 1.1.23. and Bhāṣya thereon.
12. NV, pp. 473-474.
13. PPbh, p. 423.
14. Ibid.
15. NK, p. 425.
16. Ibid, p. 426.
17. Ibid.

18. PPbh, pp. 426-427.
19. NK, p. 427.f.
20. *Vyomavatī*, pp. 122-123.
21. Ibid, p. 123.
22. Ibid.
23. Ibid.
24. PPbh, p. 428.
25. Ibid, pp. 428-429.
26. PPbh, p. 434.
27. Ibid.
28. NK, p. 434.
29. PPbh, p. 435.
30. Ibid.
31. *Vyomavatī*, p. 131; NK, p. 436; *Kiraṇāvalī*, p. 524.
32. NK, p. 437.
33. *Nyāyasāra*, p. 19 and *Nyāyabhūṣaṇa* thereon.
34. Potter, Encyclopedia of Indian Philosophies, Vol.II, p.170.
35. PPbh, pp. 436 ff.
36. Ibid, p. 438.
37. *Vyomavatī*, p. 135.
38. Ibid.
39. Ibid.
40. Ibid.
41. PPbh, pp. 439-440.
42. NK, p. 441.
43. PPbh, p. 440.
44. NS, p. 4.2.34.
45. Ibid, Bhāṣya.
46. This discussion is mainly based on Phaṇibhūṣaṇa Tarkavāgīśa, Bengali exposition on NS, 4.2.34.
47. NK, p. 627.

48. Ibid.

49. Ibid, p. 428.

50. *Vyomavatī*, p.213.

51. For example, MM, the definition of *pramā* in the first verse.

52. On SK, verse – 4.

53. NKu, 4.1.

54. NVTT, p. 35.

55. Ibid.

56. Ibid.

57. Ibid.

58. *Pariśuddhi*, p. 109.

59. Ibid, p. 110.

60. Ibid.

61. Ibid.

62. TCM, on perception, under *savikalpakavāda*.

63. NM, pt. I, p. 21.

64. Ibid.

65. Ibid.

66. NM, pt. I, pp. 95.ff.

CHAPTER SIX

Concluding Remarks

The Vaiśeṣika and the Nyāya are generally accepted as closely allied systems (*samāna-tantra*). That the two systems are on friendly terms and share the same opinions regarding various problems of metaphysics and epistemology is casily clear from the later texts. It is also a wellknown a fact that finally the two systems come to be known under a single designation called the Nyāya-Vaiśeṣika. Roughly speaking, the tendency towards syncretism becomes prominent from Udayana who belonged to the tenth century A.D.

Although the tendency is not so obvious in the case of the earlier texts of the systems, it can however be safely concluded that there is no marked antagonism between the two either. In the early Vaiśeṣika works references to the Nyāya views are naturally absent, but in Nyāya works–though not in the *Nyāyasūtra* of Gautama itself–such references are available in plenty.

In fact, examples are found as early as in the commentary of Vātsyāyana. He categorically refers to the six *padārthas* mentioned in Kaṇāda's *sūtra* and accepted by Praśastapāda. In many cases, while bringing out the implications of Gautama's *sūtras*, Vātsyāyana illustrates the point with typical Vaiśeṣika doctrines.

The author of the *Nyāyavārttika*, Uddyotakara, may be said

to go a step further. His mastery of the Vaiśeṣika theories is beyond question. He even defends the Vaiśeṣika doctrines strongly and very logically. He quotes *sūtras* from Kaṇāda's work and explains their implications. Later authors like Jayanta Bhaṭṭa, Vācaspati Miśra, Udayana and others are also no exception. They all utilize the Vaiśeṣika doctrines to a great extent while explaining the Nyāya position.

In spite of all this, however, we should not overlook the basic points of difference between the Vaiśeṣika and the Nyāya. In fact, there are, though a few, areas or problems with reference to which the two systems seem to follow different traditions. One of such areas is definitely the theories of knowledge and *pramāṇas*. If we follow the relevant portions of Praśastapāda's work we cannot but be aware of this fact.

In all the systems of Indian philosophy, *pramā* and *pramāṇa* occupy a prominent place. The definition of the different kinds of *pramā* are stated and *pramāṇas* are simply defined as their sources or instruments. Praśastapāda also follows the general line in the sense that he also gives the definitions of different forms of valid knowledge only. But his treatment of the forms of knowledge is quite different from that of the others. First he categorically states that knowledge may be valid or invalid, and then, gives a list of the specific forms of both valid and invalid cognitions. Each of them is of four types. In every other work only the valid forms are stated and defined and it is to be understood by implication that any other form of knowledge not sharing the characteristics of these is to be considered as invalid. But Praśastapāda clearly states, defines and illustrates the specific forms of knowledge considered to be invalid. He seems to give equal prominence to the discussion of both, and in fact, to the annoyance of the commentators, discusses the invalid forms of cognition first.

While enumerating the forms of valid knowledge, Praśastapāda, in agreement with general practice, of course, gives perception the first position. But here he seems to emphasise the point that for perceptual knowledge contacts among various things are essential, and such knowledge is not solely dependent upon the sense-object contact. As we have already seen, in Nyāya, the sense-object contact is given the most prominent place, though they do not deny that certain other contacts also must be there. We have also given an idea of Gautama's refutation of a part ular view (in the second chapter while critically examining perception) which is rather similar to the position maintained by Praśastapāda, and at least this view is clearly stated in Kaṇāda's *sūtra* itself.

Praśastapāda's account of perception is also distinct from those of others in that he takes up one by one the different categories admitted by the Vaiśeṣika and clearly shows how perceptual knowledge is produced in each case. He points out the exact nature of the contacts and other special factors in each case.

It is generally supposed that perception is of two kinds, namely, indeterminate and determinate. Commentators claim that these two are actually referred to in Gautama's *sūtra* and Praśastapāda's account also. However, it is difficult to be certain. Commentators might have been influenced by later interpretations. Commentators of Praśastapāda have also tried to show that the typical Nyāya theory of *upadāna-buddhi* etc. is also to be found in Praśastapāda's discussion, though here again also the fact is not so palpable.

Later Nyāya develops a special theory of perception known as *alaukika pratyakṣa*, which is divided into three forms, namely, *sāmānya-lakṣaṇa*, *jñāna-lakṣaṇa* and *yogaja*. It is obviously impossible for Praśastapāda to anticipate such intricate theories. But he at least refers to the extraordinary perception of the *yogins*, who, according to him, may be of two types. The position is followed more or less by the later authors also.

That Praśastapāda follows a distinct tradition is nowhere more apparent than in his treatment of inference. He has treated inference in great details covering all its different aspects. In fact, it is quite remarkable that for an early text like that of Praśastapāda we have such a comprehensive discussion on the topic of inference.

Praśastapāda's very definition of inference points to a different line of approach. Gautama's definition lays stress upon the fact that inference is totally dependent on perception; without a perception at its basis an inference cannot proceed at all. But Praśastapāda notes another special feature of inference, namely, that the most essential factor in the inferential process is the mark or *liṅga*.

Then he goes on to enumerate the essential properties of a valid mark, which according to him, are three, namely, the mark must be present in *pakṣa* and *sapakṣa* and must be absent from *vipakṣa*. He also expressly states that this is the view of Kaṇāda himself. As we have already mentioned, one point is here quite clear; this account bears a close resemblance with the Buddhist tradition.

In Nyāya works we do not find any such line of discussion based on the essential characteristics of the mark. Generally, in the Nyāya view, such characteristics are deduced from the enumeration of fallacious marks, which are of five kinds. It is found that each of these marks is deficient in one vital property. Therefore, logically, the absence of deficiency in respect of each property is to be regarded as the property of a valid mark. The commentators of Praśastapāda have tried their best to show that there is really no disagreement between the Nyāya and the Vaiśeṣika positions. But it is also clear that as the commentators belong to a much later period they are rather biased.

Praśastapāda's description of the inferential process also indicates difference when we compare it with the comments of Vātsyāyana on the *anumāna-sūtra*. Here Praśastapāda also refers to the view of Kaṇāda and tries to make a sort of reconciliation between his view and that of the Śāstrakāra, though scholars think that Praśastapāda has really made the significant contribution. Thus, Keith writes :

"In Praśastapāda's exposition of Kaṇāda's doctrine of inference an advance of first rate importance is made. The attempt at an exhaustive enumeration of real relations as a basis for inference is abandoned in favour of the wider conception of concomitance (*sāhacarya* in his terminology, as opposed to the later *vyāpti*) between the ground (*sahacarita*, *avinābhūta*, later *vyāpta* or *vyāpya*) and the consequence. He does not, however, admit that this is an innovation; he claims that Kaṇāda's list of real relations is not intended to be complete but illustrative, every form of relation being meant to be included. His own doctrine is simple; if anything is indissolubly connected with another in time or space it is legitimate for us, finding ourselves confronted with one of the two, to conclude the existence of the other also."

Another point which, according to scholars, goes to the great credit of Praśastapāda is the classification of inference in two types, namely, *svārtha* and *parārtha*. Most probably, this classification is not known or explicitly recognised in the early Nyāya texts, though much later it is incorporated into the Nyāya system. We may again quote Keith :

"A further important innovation is the appearance of the distinction, wholly unknown to Gautama and Kaṇāda, of the process of inference for one self (*svaniścitārtha*) and for another (*parārtha*). The distinction is one which is accepted by the syncretist school, though not adopted by commentators on the Nyāya like Uddyotakara and Vācaspati Miśra, who remain faithful to the text they explain... .

"The inference for another is definitely identified with the five-member syllogism, which in Gautama forms a category and is not classified formally as a means of proof, though inference itself is so classed".

Of course, the credit for this classification is given by some scholars to Diṅnāga also. It is difficult to fix the date of Diṅnāga with certainty. But most probably he and Praśastapāda were not far removed from each other. Scholars are divided in their opinions. According to some, Diṅnāga is senior, but others think that he is really junior. Even then, it is undeniable that Praśastapāda is the first to introduce this important classification at least into Brahmanical schools.

Praśastapāda has classified inference into two types from a different viewpoint also, namely, *dṛṣṭa* and *sāmānyato dṛṣṭa*. The first term does not occur at all in Gautama's *sūtra*, which classifies inference into three types from a quite different point of view. The second term however is there, but on the basis of Vātsyāyana's two interpretations it is clear that it means something quite different. Praśastapāda's explanation is his own.

Praśastapāda clearly states that the five *avayavas* are actually the essential components of an inference for other, which is employed to communicate a conclusion reached by one's own self. Here also the names differ from those in Nyāya except the first one. But the definition of the first is quite distinct and significant, because it is stipulated that the statement of preliminary thesis must be uncontradicted. We have already noted that this is definitely a different tradition, which does not agree with the one followed by the Nyāya, but is rather close to the one followed by the

Buddhists and the Jainas. In fact, the inclusion of this clause is significant in the sense that it suffices to exclude formulations which in the Nyāya view are supposed to be invalidated by the fallacy of the contradicted (*bādhita*).

The treatment of fallacious mark also points to the same fact. There is however a slight discrepancy. While mentioning the properties of a valid mark Praśastapāda refers to three types of fallacies corresponding to the absence of each of the three properties. However, later, when he explains and illustrates fallacious marks and their varieties he refers to an additional one. Of course, the three types are expressly stated to be admitted by Kaṇāda. The explanation of the nature of them also indicates that he is following a different tradition. He has also given a list with illustration of the different types of pseudo-instances as based on both similarity and dissimilarity, the treatment of which though available in Buddhist texts, is conspicuously absent from those in Nyāya.

Praśastapāda's classification of valid knowledge (*vidyā*) presents us with a problem. As we have already noted, according to him, the types of valid knowledge are perception (*pratyakṣa*), inference (*laiṅgika*), recollection (*smṛti*) and intuitive cognition (*ārṣa*). It is also wellknown that the term *pramāṇa* stands for the instrument of a valid knowledge. If valid knowledge is of four types, then, correspondingly, we should have also four *pramāṇas*. But, again, it is a wellknown fact that the Vaiśeṣika admits only two types of *pramāṇa*, namely, perception and inference. Therefore, the question arises what would be the nature of the instruments of the other two types of valid knowledge? In the text itself or in the commentaries we do not find any reference either to the problem or its solution.

It is perhaps not difficult to explain the case of intuitional cognition. The concept of the three types of extraordinary contacts (*alaukika-sannikarṣa*) has not naturally developed in the time of Praśastapāda. But there is no doubt that he has admitted the extraordinary perception of the yogin. He has said that intuitive cognition is generally possible in the case of seers who has reached a high state of perfection, and it is very rarely possible in the case of an ordinary person. Thus, such knowledge may somehow be considered an extraordinary form of perception and thereby its instrument may well be accepted as *pratyakṣa-pramāṇa*.

The case of recollection is quite different. According to the author of the text, it is valid knowledge, but none of the commentators accept it to be so. If the position of the commentators which follows the general line of thought in Indian philosophy is accepted, then, there is practically no problem, though it is not clear how such a position can be maintained against the expressly stated view of the author of the text. Thus, if we try to remain faithful to him, how are we to explain the nature of the instrument of recollection? We must remember that the instrument must be either perception or inference, if we are to remain faithful to the Vaiśeṣika tradition. But in the text itself there is no hint. As the object of recollection is not present there at the time the knowledge is produced it cannot be a case of perception. Again, in the case of inference, the object may or may not be there, but still it requires a lot of other factors, e.g. a mark, invariable concomitance etc.. As such factors are not available in the case of recollection it is rather difficult to accept it as a form of inferential cognition.

It is perhaps rather strange that all the commentators should be so much up against the validity of recollection. Recollection is said to be a kind of invalid knowledge, but it is observed that recollective cognition is vitally necessary in the case of the three other types of valid knowledge other than perception. One of the grounds of inference is the knowledge of concomitance. But in the process of inference such knowledge is only recollective in nature. In the case of knowledge derived through comparison (*upamiti*), one of the essential factors, namely, the knowledge of the meaning of *atideśa-vākya*, is again a sort of recollection. Lastly, *śabda-bodha* also is dependent upon the recollective cognition of the meanings expressed by the words uttered. In other words, we have to admit that invalid knowledge is a means for valid knowledge.

In this connection it would not perhaps be irrelevant to note briefly some points raised by the Jainas who are the only Indian philosophers to admit categorically that recollection is definitely a form of valid knowledge and moreover defend the position with elaborate arguments.

It has been argued that so far as the object of recollection is concerned, it is totally dependent on a previous perception. Inference is so dependent only for its genesis, but it is independent so far as its object is concerned.

The Jainas counter the argument by saying that, like recollection, inference also is not an independent source, because it does no more than establish a fact which has already been proved by the establishment of the invariable concomitance between *hetu* and *sādhya*.

It may be argued that the ascertainment establishing the invariable concomitance deals with a general truth, but the inference establishes a concrete case. So inference may be called an independent process. As against this, the Jainas point out that the previous experience which lies at the basis of recollection gives the knowledge of an object with many details, but recollection gives a knowledge of the object with but a small number of details, and hence, it also represents an independent process.

It is also pointed out that if recollection is not accepted to be valid, then the validity of a persistent cognition (*dhāravāhika-jñāna*) also cannot be established. In such a case also only the first cognition of the series would be valid. But as the subsequent cognitions reveal the same object it becomes very much similar to recollective cognition, and as such, should not be accepted as valid.

Praśastapāda's contribution lies in the fact that he presents us with a commendable account of the Vaiśeṣika theory of knowledge. We have already shown on different occasions that not much concrete information is available in the *Vaiśeṣikasūtra* of Kaṇāda. The discussion of the topics is not well planned, and often information is scattered here and there. But Praśastapāda's presentation is definite, clear, coherent and logically arranged. Sometimes his remarks are brief and may not be easy to understand, still generally his intentions are clear and well-phrased. This account is valuable not only for a clear idea of the Vaiśeṣika theory of knowledge, it is also important as a source-book for the study of ancient Indian theories of knowledge in general, and also particularly for a comparative study of the position of the early Buddhists.

Abbreviations

AS	–	Arthaśāstra.
ASILM	–	Advanced Studies in Indian Logic & Metaphysics.
BP	–	Bhāṣāpariccheda.
HB	–	Hetubindu.
HBT	–	Hetubinduṭīkā.
KKK	–	Khaṇḍanakhaṇḍakhādya.
MM	–	Mānameyodaya.
NB	–	Nyāyabindu.
NBT	–	Nyāyabinduṭīkā.
NK	–	Nyāyakandalī.
NKu	–	Nyāyakusumāñjali.
NM	–	Nyāyamañjarī.
NS	–	Nyāyasūtra.
NV	–	Nyāyavārttika.
NVTT	–	Nyāyavārttikātatparyaṭīkā.
PKM	–	Prameyakamalamārtaṇḍa.
PM	–	Pramāṇamīmāṃsā.
PP	–	Prakaraṇapañcikā.
PPbh	–	Praśastapādabhāṣya.
PS	–	Pramāṇasamuccaya.
SDS	–	Sarvadarśanasaṃgraha.
SK	–	Sāṅkhyakārikā.

SM	–	Siddhāntamuktāvalī.
SV	–	Ślokavārttika.
SVR	–	Syādvādaratnākara.
TB	–	Tarkabhāṣā.
TCM	–	Tattvacintāmaṇi.
TSV	–	Tattvārthaśloka-vārttika.
VP	–	Vākyapadīya.
VS	–	Vaiśeṣikasūtra.

Select Bibliography

Advanced studies in Indian Logic & Metaphysics, Sukhlalji Sanghvi, Calcutta, 1961.

Arthaśāstra (Kauṭilya), text and English tr. ed. R.P. Kangle, Bombay, 1960.

Ātmatattvaviveka (Udayana) with the comments of Nārāyaṇa, Raghunātha and

Gadādhara, ed. Paṇḍit Ḍhuṇḍhiraja Śāstri, Benares, 1940.

Bhartṛhari: A study of the Vākyapadīya in the light of the ancient commentaries, K.A.S. Iyer, Poona, 1969.

Bhāṣāpariccheda of Viśvanātha, (1) with commentaries by author (Muktāvalī). Dinakara and Ramarudra, ed. Ātmarāma Śarmā, Bombay, 1933. (2) with

Muktāvalī, Prabhā and Mañjuṣā commentaries, ed. C.S.R.Śāstri, Madras, 1923.

The Encyclopaedia of Indian Philosophies, vol. II, ed. Karl H. Potter, Delhi 1977.

Hetubindu (Dharmakīrti), Sanskrit text as given in the supplement to HBT.

Hetubindu-ṭīkā (Arcaṭa), with commentary by Durveka Miśra, Baroda, 1949.

A History of Indian Logic, Satis Chandra Vidyabhushana Delhi, 1971.

A History of Indian Philosophy, Surendranath Dasgupta, in 5 vols, Delhi, 1975.

Indian Logic and Atomism, A.B. Keith, New Delhi, 1974.

Indian Philosophy : A Popular Introduction, Debiprasad Chattopadhyaya, New Delhi, 1972.

Khaṇḍana-Khaṇḍa-Khādya (Śrīharṣa). (1) with commentary by Śaṃkara Miśra, ed. Navikanta Jha, Varansi, 1970, (2) with vidyāsāgarī commentary, ed. Svami Yogindrananda, Varanasi, 1979.

Kiraṇāvalī (Udayana), ed. Narendra Chandra Vedantatirtha, (reprint), Calcutta, 2002.

Mānameyodaya (Nārāyaṇa Bhaṭṭa and Nārāyaṇa Paṇḍita), ed. C.K. Raja and S.S.S. Sastri, Madras, 1933.

Nyāyabindu (Dharmakīrti), with commentary by Dharmottara, ed. C.S. Shastri, Benares, 1924.

Nyāyabhāṣya of Vātsyāyana, see NS.

Nyāyabhūṣana, auto-commentary on Nyāyasāra (Bhāsarvajña), ed. Svāmi Yogindrananda, Varanasi, 1968.

Nyāyadarśana, ed. Phaṇibhūṣaṇa Tarkavāgīśa, 5 vols, Sūtra, Bhāṣya and detailed exposition, Calcutta, 1324-1336 (Bengali year).

Nyāyakandalī (Śrīdhara), see Praśastapādabhāṣya.

Nyāyakusumāñjali (Udayana), (1) With auto-commentary and four sub-commentaries, ed. Padmaprasād Upādhyāya and Dhuṇḍhirāja Śāstri, Vārāṇasī, 1957. (2) With Haridāsī commentary, ed. Nārāyaṇa Miśra, Varansi.

Nyāyalīlāvati (Vallabhācārya), with commentaries by Vardhamāna, Śaṅkara Miśra and Bhagīratha Ṭhakkura, Benares.

Nyāyamañjarī (Jayanta Bhaṭṭa), ed. S.N. Sukla, Varanasi, 1971.

Nyāya Philosophy, Debiprasad Chattopadhyaya and

Mrinanlkanti Gangopadhyaya, Parts I-V, Calcutta, 1967-1976.

Nyāyasūtra or Nyāyadarśana (Gautama), with Bhāṣya, Vārttika, Tātparyaṭīkā and Nyāya Vṛtti, Calcutta, 1936.

Nyāyasūtravivaraṇa (Rādhāmohana Gosvāmin) ed. Surendralal Tarkatirtha, Benares, 1903.

Nyāyasūtravṛtti (Viśvanātha). See NS.

Nyāyavārttika (Uddyotakara). See NS.

Nyāyavārtikatātparyaṭīkā or Tātparyaṭīkā (Vācaspati Miśra). See NS.

Nyāyavārttikātatparyaṭīkāpariśuddhi (Udayana), Vol. I. ed. Anantalal Thakur, Darbhanga.

Outlines of Indian Philosophy, M. Hiriyanna, Bombay, 1973.

Praśastapādabhāṣya or Padārthadharmasaṅgraha (Praśastapāda), (1) with Nyāyakandalī, ed. Durgādhar Jha, Varanasi, 1963 Eng. tr. by Ganganatha Jha, Benaras, 1916; (2) with NK and three sub-commentaries there on, R. T. Vyas, Vadodara, 1991.

Sarvadarśanasaṃgraha (Mādhavācārya), Poona, 1928.

Siddhāntamuktāvalī or Muktāvalī (Viśvanātha), See Bhāṣāpariccheda.

Sāṃkhyakārikā (Īśvarakṛṣṇsna), with Yuktidīpikā commentary, ed. R.S. Tripathi, Varanasi, 1970.

Studies in the History of Indian Philosophy. An anthology of articles by scholars Easrern, and Western, ed. Debiprasad Chattopadhyaya, Calcutta, 1978.

Ślokavārttika (Kumārila Bhaṭṭa), ed. Svami Dvarikādās Śāstrī, Varansi, 1978.

Syādvādaratnākara (Vādidevasūri), ed. Motilal Ladhaji, Vol. 2, Pune, Vīrasaṃvat 2453.

Tātparyaṭīkā, commentary on NV, See NVTT.

Tattvacintāmaṇi (Pramālakṣaṇa) (1) ed. Biśvabandhu Bhattacharyya, Calcutta, 2000; (2) (Gaṅgeśa), ed. Kāmākhyānātha Tarkavāgīśa, Calcutta, 1892.

Upāyahṛdaya (attributed to Nāgārjuna) in Pre-Diṅnāga Buddhist texts on Logic from Chinese sources, ed. G.Tucci, Baroda, 1930.

Upaskāra (Śaṅkara Miśra), see VS.

Vākyapadīya (Bhartṛhari), with Vṛtti and Paddhati commentary of Vṛṣabhadeva, ed. K.A.S. Iyer, Poona, 1966; Eng. tr. K.A.S. Iyer, Poona, 1965.

Vaiśeṣikasūtra (Kaṇāda), (1) with Upaskāra commentary, ed. Nārāyaṇa Miśra, Varanasi, 1969; (2) with the commentary of Candrānandra, ed. Jambuvijayaji, Baroda, 1982.

Vyomavatī (Vyomaśivācārya), commentary on Praśastapādabhāṣya, (1) ed.

Gopinath Kaviraj and Dhuṇḍhirāja Śāstri, Benares, 1930; (2) ed. Gourinath Sastri, parts I and II, Varanasi 1983-1984.